# WHEN KINGDOMS CLASH

P E A C E · A N D · J U S T I C E · S E R I E S  6

# WHEN KINGDOMS CLASH

## The Christian and Ideologies

# CALVIN E. SHENK

HERALD PRESS
Scottdale, Pennsylvania
Kitchener, Ontario

146739

**Library of Congress Cataloging-in-Publication Data**

Shenk, Calvin E., 1936-
    When kingdoms clash : the Christian and ideologies / Calvin E.
Shenk.
       p.   cm. — (Peace and justice series ; 6)
    Bibliography: p.
    ISBN 0-8361-3481-8 (pbk.)
    1. Sociology, Christian.   2. Ideology—Religious aspects-
-Christianity.   I. Title.   II. Series.
BT738.S52  1988                             88-14719
261.2—dc19                                  CIP

Cover photograph by David Hiebert of the June 12, 1982, march for
nuclear disarmament in New York City.

Unless otherwise indicated, Scripture quotations are from the *Good
News Bible*. Old Testament copyright © American Bible Society 1976;
New Testament copyright © American Bible Society 1966, 1971, 1976.

WHEN KINGDOMS CLASH
Copyright © 1988 by Herald Press, Scottdale, Pa. 15683
    Published simultaneously in Canada by Herald Press,
    Kitchener, Ont. N2G 4M5. All rights reserved.
Library of Congress Catalog Card Number: 88-14719
International Standard Book Number: 0-8361-3481-8
Printed in the United States of America
Design by Gwen Stamm/Paula M. Johnson

1 2 3 4 5 6 7 8 96 95 94 93 92 91 90 89 88

*To friends in Africa*
*who by modeling Christian faith*
*in the midst of conflicting ideologies*
*have become my teachers.*

# Contents

# Foreword

Different systems of thought compete for our attention wherever we live. These ideologies help to organize society for specific purposes. The goals are usually intended to benefit human beings by structuring life in an orderly manner.

Sometimes, however, the people who put these ideologies into practice abuse their power. They lose sight of the goal—to benefit the people. The ideology which was originally intended for good then becomes evil.

In *When Kingdoms Clash* author Calvin Shenk identifies a few of the major ideologies of our time. After briefly explaining them, he shows how the church can learn from these systems of thought. One way is to examine them in light of Scripture. He shows how "faith judges all ideologies."

The kingdom of God begun by Jesus judges all other political, economic, and social systems. "It crowds them out of first place," he says. Christians can therefore work in any situation, regardless of the prevailing ideology.

The author brings to his writing both training in missions and world religions and teaching experience in the U.S., Ethiopia, Israel, and India. As one who has lived in areas with widely differing ideologies, he is able to draw on his broad experience to illustrate key points. His brief statement on ideologies offers valuable insights for Christians whose first loyalty is to "a kingdom not of this world."

Because of this loyalty, Christians look beyond the borders of their own nation. As the author says, "Christians are, first of all, world citizens." This concern for all people gives us a clearer vision of how to live in our particular place and time.

*When Kingdoms Clash* is volume six in a series on peace and justice themes. Mennonite Board of Missions, Mennonite Publishing House, and the Peace Sections of the Board of Congregational Ministries and Mennonite Central Committee—all Mennonite agencies—commissioned the series. The series bridges a gap between scholarly Mennonite writings and narrowly focused evangelical literature that talks peace while neglecting discipleship. Persons wanting to pursue the theme further may check the references listed in "For Further Reading and Study" near the end of the book.

—*J. Allen Brubaker, Editor*
*Peace and Justice Series*

# *Preface*

In September 1974, Haile Selassie I of Ethiopia was deposed from the throne he occupied for more than forty years. This revolution ended centuries of rule by an emperor and introduced a political and social reality based mainly on Marxist-Socialist ideas. It soon became obvious that the position of the church was also changing.

During the first stages of the revolution, I was teaching at Mekane Yesus (Lutheran) Seminary in Addis Ababa. The church sought to respond to this change in political leadership by studying the gospel and the new political concepts. A seminar was convened at the seminary on the gospel and socialism. One of the important models in that discussion was the Chinese experience. Later I taught a course at the seminary on ideologies (systems of thought for shaping society). I also helped to educate people in the church to the new social reality.

My experience in a developing African nation that sought to apply Marxist socialism therefore influenced my thinking. Marxism is one of the two (along with capitalism) principal contenders for the loyalty of people in the world.

During this century it has provided the greatest challenge to Christian faith. Marxism is a well-defined ideology and can therefore assist us in *evaluating* the others. I will also draw many illustrations from the experience of the church in China.

The clash of kingdoms is increasing in our world as old structures crumble. The church can never isolate itself from this turmoil. It needs to face new situations, guided by God's commands and promises. Only then can it carefully assess its limitations and opportunities.

*—Calvin E. Shenk*

# CHAPTER 1

# *Definition and Function of Ideologies*

What is an ideology and why is this important for Christians to understand?

An ideology, or system of thought, is a plan for shaping society and interpreting history. An ideology may seek to defend the existing social structures or it may attempt to change them. Ideologies create collective human awareness. Ideologies combine theory with action and try to get people to participate in shaping their own destiny. Ideologies contain strategies and methods to bridge the gap between the idea and the fulfillment of it. They give meaning to people's lives, inspire visions for the future, and try to enable people to realize that vision.

From another perspective, ideology is a kind of awareness, a social consensus, a cultural system, a worldview. Every society has some ideology as its foundation. Everyone, consciously or unconsciously, is involved in a particular economic or political ideology. This, in turn, has a strong impact upon attitudes, values, and behavior. The social climate created by the ideology permeates our lives because it is embodied in political parties, schools, the military, and the media.

Governments often become the instrument for an ideology. Every nation pledges loyalty to an ideology which serves its interests. While ideology is closely related to nationalism, nationalism is often stronger than the ideology.

All of us need to increase our awareness of the impact of ideology in our own contexts. What are the main ideas and concerns which give shape and pattern to life in our society? What is the dominant ideology? What does it perceive as its role? How does the ideology exert pressure? To what extent do faith communities participate in shaping dominant ideas in the society?

Within some societies there is more than one ideology. One of these may reflect the interest of a dominant class by justifying its power, prestige, and privilege. While those in power may have one ideology (apartheid in South Africa), the dominated may have another (African nationalism, black consciousness in South Africa). When those in power and those seeking power collide, the dominant exert more force.

Ideologies can also help break down the division between classes. In societies where this happens, ideologies are not necessarily linked to a specific group interest.

Some ideologies claim relevance for all societies. For example, followers of Marx make such a claim for Marxism. About one-half of the world's population lives under its influence. Other ideologies propose a way of life for a particular society, nation, or movement (African socialism in Tanzania). Ideologies said to be universal compete with each other, both within societies and between them. Each seeks followers through endless propaganda. Each makes global claims for its own values, its unique place in history, and its destiny for all humanity.

All of us are familiar with the tension between the rather well-defined ideologies of the West and of the Marxist-socialist world. Less well-known are some of the ideologies of the so-called third world. The third world faces issues of nation building. These include the balance between authority and freedom, economic growth, social change, and new cultural practices. Those in power and those seeking power use ideology for their own purposes.

Third-world ideologies are preoccupied with national liberation, national unity, national security, or national development. Some ideologies are borrowed from larger systems and modified to suit a national purpose. Others emerge from the particular national context. Ideologies may draw their strengths from capitalism, socialism, religion, particular ethnic groups, local culture, or concern for the national security state.

Ideologies can easily become total systems. They then claim to be the sole authority in all essential social spheres to control the people. Ideologies seek to explain all facts in a consistent way. Yet they have at best just some of the facts. Certain facts are omitted and other ideas are created or imagined in order to build a coherent system. In an attempt to be convincing, ideologies often try to exercise complete control.

When an ideology becomes the total reality, it is no longer a symbol but an idol. A symbol can help to explain the world and even liberate it. An idol, however, veils the real world and leads to oppression. Too often as ideologies try to answer the most important human questions, they become like religion. Or they place absolute value upon nation, class, race, culture, security, or revolution. We are familiar with the evils of Nazism as a state-controlled system in Germany. And we object to the abuses of certain forms of Marxism as a total ideology.

We can consider an ideology good when it serves as a plan to reach just goals. But we consider an ideology harmful when it serves itself or specific interests or systems of injustice. As a system, it can so easily distort the truth. Ideologies may inspire hope (land reform, liberation) as well as conflict. Differing ideologies offer rival hopes, but too often those hopes are not fully achieved. For example, Marxism promises justice for all; capitalism promises freedom for all.

*Ideology is false when it makes part of the reality the total reality.* Partial truth may never become the total truth. We must discern between the true and the false.

# CHAPTER 2

# *Kinds of Ideologies*

From the many kinds of ideologies, the several selected here illustrate the character of ideology. We will not be able to provide a full treatment or evaluation of any of these for lack of space. We must remember, too, that ideologies vary within and between particular political and social situations. Some national ideologies combine elements from different systems. Certain ideologies produce counterideologies. When ideologies belong to a larger system, the local environment shapes their specific expression.

## *Marxist-Socialist Ideology*

Karl Marx developed one of the most well-thought-out ideologies, with a unified vision and plan for action. Marx's fundamental conviction was that humans were less than they could be because they lived and worked in a middle-class, capitalist society. This theory of alienation is the focal point of his entire philosophy. People were separated from themselves, from the work process, and from others. When humans are valued for their economic benefit, they are mistreated and their worst appetites are encouraged. Marx insisted therefore that the social structure must be completely changed.

Marx believed that people shape history by the way they use resources, knowledge, and skills to produce goods. History has shown that as this process developed, people oppressed others and formed classes. In this materialistic view of history, people who control the forces of production form one class (capitalists), and those who provide the labor form another (the proletariat).

Marx believed the oppressed must struggle with the oppressors to gain control of the means of production. They must abolish all classes. This will happen when the oppressed overthrow the established order and liberate themselves and the oppressors.

Marx was not content merely to interpret the world; he wanted to change it. His goal was the perfect community, the communist society. It would replace the injustice of other political and social systems. He believed one could accomplish this if the whole community owned and controlled the means of production—capital, land, property. Thus the community could manage these in the interests of everyone. A revolution was needed, however, to create this social unity and to do away with class distinctions.

*Socialism*

Socialism advocates community or state ownership and management of the means of production and distribution of goods and services. It takes different forms, however, throughout the world. For example, Marxist socialisms are in the Soviet Union, Eastern Europe, China, North Korea, Vietnam, Cuba, and Ethiopia. Arab socialisms are in Al-

geria and Egypt. African socialisms appear in Guinea, So-
malia, and Tanzania. Scandinavia sports a democratic socialism.

Democratic socialism has socialist features. These include the public control and planning of the economy for
more equal distribution of social wealth and social security.
At the same time it encourages private enterprise. This
"mixed economy" provides a balance between competition, private initiative, and overall planning. Liberal democratic institutions are respected.

## Democratic Capitalism

As an ideology, capitalism allows individuals to own the
means of production. The power of production is shared
among many property owners rather than held by one
owner, the state. Capitalism holds that progress happens
more rapidly under private ownership because profits encourage maximum output. The foundation of capitalism is
free enterprise and free competition. These depend upon a
free market regulated by the balance between supply and
demand, rather than state control.

Under capitalism, free individuals make their own economic decisions in light of their interests, experience, and
intelligence. Workers can choose their own line of work
and their particular job. Businessmen can choose their type
of business and investors can invest their capital wherever
they choose. The consumer can buy the product preferred.
The planning process is guided by competition, the profit
principle, and the buying patterns of the consumer, rather
than the state. Capitalism supposedly improves the quality
of work and the efficiency of production.

Individual freedom is the foundation of capitalism.

Equality, responsibility, and opportunity are important concepts. Each person has the right and the duty to develop his or her own potential. Humans are believed to be basically good and are free to pursue individual happiness and self-interests. They are masters of their own destiny and of reality. If each chooses for self, society as a whole will benefit.

*Ideology of the National Security State*

José Comblin has described the ideology that has developed in some parts of Latin America as the "national security state." Comblin argues that the national security state revolves around power. The survival of the nation is the absolute good and the chief object of every citizen's life. People become agents of the will of the state. For the sake of national security, people are denied individual liberties. Economic development becomes a tool for national security. The national security state is controlled by the military elite. They defend their self-appointed leadership as necessary to prevent a Marxist takeover or extremist subversion.

The national security state, instead of creating social stability, often causes tensions and insecurity. Constitutions and congresses are abolished and replaced by new institutions which need a new ideology. Though this ideology is not carefully spelled out, it spreads throughout nations and the world. As a totalitarian power, it redefines the meaning of human existence. Every citizen is subject to rigid state control.

Many of the characteristics of the national security states of Latin America exist in the rightist regimes of South Korea, Taiwan—and, until recently, the Philippines. For example, the South Korean government has justified recent political repression on the basis of security and economic development. The presence of the hostile regime in the North is used for political clout in the South.

## Religion as Ideology

In recent years, we have seen an increase in non-Christian religions. Such religions often gain strength through the rise of local cultures and the nationalism that follows. Because many cultures are thought to weaken national unity, one religion sometimes emerges to defend the political and economic belief system. Even when religion is not the state religion, it may receive protection and favors from the government.

There are many examples of religious ideology. Many Muslims understand religion and state as a total social entity. Islam therefore becomes a kind of ideology. All of us have some awareness of the impact of Islam on the national ideology of Iran, Libya, and Saudi Arabia. Buddhism has a profound effect upon the ideology of Burma, Sri Lanka, and Tibet. In Nepal, Hinduism is the state religion, and in India, Hinduism is gaining a more dominant role.

## Apartheid

Apartheid is an ideology of separation in South Africa. It emerged from the nationalism of Afrikaners, white South Africans of Dutch descent who speak Afrikaans.

Based on their own desire for separation and ethnic identity, Afrikaners argued for the self-determination of all peoples in South Africa. Self-determination suggests that each group of people has the right to maintain its independence from other groups of people. Apartheid enforces rigid separation of people based upon race. Afrikaners believe their identity is threatened by mixing with people of African or Asian origin. They use structure and power to mobilize people in terms of self-determination and race. These structures resemble a national security state, for the white minority controls the black majority in order to guarantee their own security.

Apartheid is a policy of divide and rule. Whites deny blacks full participation in society and limit their freedoms. Apartheid is a religious ideology. It uses Scripture to promote separate development (tower of Babel, Genesis 11). Although apartheid is closely linked with the economic power of capitalism, it shares wealth, power, and prestige unevenly.

## Zionism

Zionism gave rise to the modern state of Israel. Zionism developed from the efforts of many Jews to achieve a political, cultural, and religious identity of their own. Although influenced by nationalism, Zionism expresses the religious understanding of "a chosen people for a chosen land." One cannot understand Zionism apart from Hitler's killing of the Jews and the Jewish fight for survival. Secular and religious Jews find a common identity in Zionism. The Jewish religion has an impact upon Israeli culture beyond the proportion of religious Jews. Zionism continues to define itself in relation to Palestinian counterideologies.

# CHAPTER 3

# *Ideologies and Religion*

Some ideologies oppose religion while others seek to gain its support. Some, themselves religious, want to exclude competing religions. Others guarantee freedom of religion. However, ideology usually wants to control or use religion because religion competes for people's loyalty and seldom tolerates other loyalties.

*Criticism of and Opposition to Religion*

The ideology most representative of this position is Marxism. Marx, Engels, Lenin, and Mao Tse-tung were all atheists. Atheism is a denial of both God's existence and his dominion. Marxists have opposed religion for reasons which follow.

First, they regard religion as submission to authority. Marxists believe that to be fully human one must be self-determined, free, and guided by reason. Only atheism is rational. Faith in God must be replaced by faith in humans. Mao declared that China "had no other god but the Chinese people." According to Marxists, God is a projection of human self-consciousness, a result of the imagination. The more humans trust God the less they regard themselves. This leads to an unhealthy dependence.

Second, they criticize religion as a reflection of human misery and an obstacle to social change. Religion is a symptom that something is wrong, a sign of a much deeper problem. It's the "sigh of a tormented creature." The deeper problem, Marxists say, is economics and power structures. Religion tries to change the inner feelings of people without changing the structures. Religion is on the side of reaction. Religion causes alienation, for people look to God and neglect their neighbor. Religion accommodates the views of the ruling classes. It is a survival of the capitalist past.

Third, they consider religion an evil illusion, a false ideology, unrealistic in its idealism. Religion is a fantasy by which humans cheat themselves. God becomes the perfection of what they are not able to perfect. According to Marxists, humans make religion; religion does not make humans. Consciousness does not determine life; life determines consciousness. Religion is an opium used by the ruling classes to oppress the poor. Religion takes people's minds off their suffering in the world. Marx believed people would not really be happy until religion disappeared because people who dream of another world will not change this one. In the classless society of the future, Marx thought, human possibilities will be realized and God will not be needed.

Fourth, Marxists say religion is simply a false substitute for science. It has an unscientific and superstitious view of the world that is harmful to human welfare. Religion arises because humans fear uncontrollable forces. But science takes the mystery out of nature. Humans no longer need to worship that which is within their control. Religion will disappear when human needs are adequately met.

Fifth, Marxists hold that religion must be eliminated. Some believe history is on the side of atheism, so religion will eventually vanish and die. Others see religion as an opposing force and actively combat it. They use antireligious propaganda, restriction, and persecution. Lenin was militant against religion, as were the Red Guards of the Chinese cultural revolution. Albania and North Korea have also actively oppressed religion.

Though Marxists are critical of religion, some have reevaluated it. Today, the practice in Marxist-socialist states varies considerably. Often we see a swing between a "hard" and a "soft" line. Within a given state variations may exist between the policies of the central government and the regions, or between regions. Likewise, policies change in different periods of history. Sometimes the shift in the Marxist attitude toward religion emerges from within the ideology. At other times, a shift occurs when the church softens its attitude toward the ideology. For example, when believers in Hungary involved themselves in drug and alcohol rehabilitation programs, the authorities gradually relaxed restrictions.

Marxists use different strategies at different times. They have learned that they cannot eliminate religion by force. Indeed, persecution has led to a revival of religion. In many cases, the government grants more freedom of religion. However, among Marxists, understandings of freedom of religion differ. For many, freedom of religion means freedom to believe in one's heart or freedom to worship in specified places under certain conditions. Religious activity outside of church buildings or social service activities are either prohibited or regulated. Repressive governments want religion to be private.

Since religion is still considered an outdated worldview, antireligious propaganda may continue. Some Marxists, however, have de-emphasized the spreading of atheism. For example, the most recent Chinese constitution has removed the phrase "to propagate atheism." Yet the line between permitted religious activities and prohibited "superstition" is thin. Believers are denied higher education and employment in the professions. Such pressure may be indirect through economic isolation or reward for unbelief.

In some societies, we see a move from hostility to restriction or reluctant tolerance. We may even find some Marxists who practice religion, such as in India. Marxists may openly admit mistakes. I remember my surprise on hearing a former Red Guard expressing regret to our group in China for earlier improper behavior. Many of us recall the hard times in China when the authorities took over church institutions and religious organizations could not function. Literature was taken and destroyed. Religious buildings were used for other purposes. Religious professionals had to get other jobs. Later, Christians were tolerated more, but the state called on the church to demonstrate patriotism by active support of the system.

Some Marxist-socialist states suggest that religion can contribute to social harmony in building a new society. After political revolutions, new regimes may invite religion to serve the state in the process of socialization. For example, Stalin discovered the church was a strong support in time of war. But the new toleration seen in many societies requires that religion not engage in counterrevolutionary activities or disrupt public order. It may not interfere in social, political, or international affairs.

The party has supreme power, and opposition is illegal. It may grant concessions to the secondary aspects of religion but not on the ideological level. Religion is still subject to the state, and the church must carefully observe limits imposed by the state. When religion competes with the state for people's loyalty it is considered subversive.

When the church's loyalty to the state is suspect, swift retribution may follow. At one point, Mozambique accused the church of turning people against socialism and closed churches and religious institutions. (This was later modified.) Angola provided religious freedom as long as it did not oppose the state's ideology. Since churches had helped in the Angolan liberation struggle, the government enlisted its help in nation building. The Christian can only welcome this greater toleration so long as the church is not manipulated.

## Attempts to Gain the Support of Religion

In the national security states of Latin America and in the rightist regimes of Asia one finds no official persecution of religion. At first these states appear quite accepting of religion and the church. But such rightist governments encourage a culture religion which defends the policies of the government. The regimes expect from the church a type of presence and action which fits in with the established economic, social, political, and ideological system. Their leaders want a church which encourages the people to support the state, a religion that fights communism. The use of religion by rightist ideologies is very subtle.

Until recently, one could easily equate the goals and objectives of the state in Latin America with those of the church because both needed mutual protection and support. This situation is changing now. Yet military governments claim to defend Christian principles, and in crises call upon religion to help preserve the system.

The national security state wants to work with the church to defend democracy and Christianity. Its advocates do not see the contradictions between their theories and Christianity. Rather, they believe their ideology gives the church an important part in society and enables it to have more influence than in any other ideological system. They are offended when the church refuses to assist the state to fight communism or to build a new society.

Some parts of the church enjoy a privileged position and want to fight communism. They participate in building a new society and believe evangelization of the masses depends upon increasing the influence of the church in society. A growing number of Christians, however, are concerned about social injustice and question the role of the church in blessing the ideology.

In South Korea the church has freedom to proclaim the gospel, but in the name of security, the state has placed restrictions on it. It has harassed the church for speaking against oppressive measures of the government. It therefore has tried to eliminate opposition without creating an impression of religious persecution. The government justifies actions against the church because of unacceptable political behavior rather than religious behavior.

Apartheid is in many ways a "Christian heresy" because supporters have used elements of Christian faith to develop and promote this ideology. It is a type of civil religion used to bless the state in the name of national security.

In contexts of national security, the ideology easily takes

over religion. When that happens, the church often neglects the social aspects of faith to maintain its freedom.

### Religious Ideologies Which Restrict Christian Faith

Religious ideologies also make an impact on Christian faith. In some countries it is a civil offense to change one's religion without legal process. When there are several religions, the government may oppose efforts to change people from one religion to another. Its leaders may fear that hostility and violence will develop between the different religious groups. Such conflict is harmful to national unity.

Since Muslims understand religion and state as one entity, other religions are a threat to national unity. Iran and Pakistan make life difficult for non-Muslims. Saudi Arabia does not permit congregations of non-Muslims to exist. Other Muslim states may not provide enough protection for religious minorities or they may ignore existing constitutional protection. Within Muslim states, freedom of religion varies, but is to some degree restricted.

Buddhism is a state religion in several countries, but the degree of religious freedom varies. Conversion of Hindus to Christianity is forbidden in the Hindu Kingdom of Nepal. Since it is against the law for Hindus to change their religion, public evangelism is a great offense.

Orthodox Jews in Israel use their influence to suppress Christianity among the non-Arab populations. Jews who believe in Jesus experience harassment.

### Freedom of Religion in Democratic Capitalist Contexts

Democratic-capitalist societies guarantee freedom of religion in their constitutions. Some insist on separation of

church and state (United States). Others have a state
church (Great Britain). Each, however, wants to provide
for freedom and equality for all religious groups.

Several tendencies are apparent in these societies. In
some instances, religion functions on the edge of society,
and secularism has emerged as a new kind of ideology. Religion has not disappeared completely, but it has lost its
major role in cultural development. As Joseph Kitgawa
said, "We operate with a *Time* magazine approach to religion; religion is a little section of life between theater and
sport." Secularism makes religion seem unnecessary. Religious indifference becomes a kind of atheism. Religion is
not opposed, but regarded as obsolete.

In the midst of this secularism, a new civil religion ap-
pears. This God-and-country religion supports the existing
ideology.

*Conclusion*

We have seen that ideological systems may fear the
church's impact upon its members or welcome its support.
Even where governments permit religious freedom, they
expect churches to mind faith and ignore politics. Religious
freedom is for religious activities, not political activities.
The only political activity welcomed is that which rein-
forces the ideology.

However, religion, like nationalism, is not easily sub-
dued. Ideologies often underestimate its passion. Yet the
nature of all ideologies is to want to control. Given this fact,
the church must be perceptive. There is always the danger
that the church will be taken over, used, and finally cast
aside.

# CHAPTER 4

# *The Church Learns from Ideologies*

The church must develop alertness to the ideologies under which it lives. Then it can listen and learn from them without being conquered by them. The church has often been self-righteous, becoming more so when confronted by ideology. Marxists think the church is a captive of false self-understanding.

Criticism can drive us deeper into the Bible and give us fresh insight in our reading of it. We may then discover that some of our understandings have been more cultural than biblical. We need sincere self-criticism, not just empty gestures to create a better self-image. We need to acknowledge our mistakes and repent. In October 1986, the white Dutch Reformed Church admitted that

> the forced separation of people cannot be seen as a prescription of the Bible but is an error that must be rejected. . . . The Church is convinced that the use of apartheid as a sociopolitical system . . . cannot be accepted on Christian ethical grounds because it militates against the principle of brotherly love and justice and inevitably affects the human dignity of those involved.

Let us hope that such self-criticism can lead to genuine change.

## The Church Admits Failure

We need not accept all criticism as true. We must, however, find our way between rejection of criticism and naive acceptance of it. Honest self-criticism does not mean that we are always on the defensive. We must also take the offensive. We must expose ideological myths, for they cannot provide all the answers.

Yet, the church has too often been allied with economic, racial, and political power. It has supported economic interests above people's needs and accepted as lawful the abuse of power. Sometimes this occurred openly. At other times it was implied. In many places, the church has identified with the middle class and sided with the ruling class, supporting the existing order, even when unjust. By becoming defensive, it has sometimes been an obstacle to the processes of change in history. People have preferred law and order over change. The church has sometimes forced on others this power thus gained or held.

Even the cross has become a symbol of power in some areas. For example, the effect of such power was experienced in China as "a religion of love spread by force." The Chinese Revolution later showed that Christians were a privileged people allied with power.

Can we learn detachment from manipulative power? Can truth and power be disentangled? Walter Sawatsky, a scholar in East-West relations, once asked, "How thorough is our conversion from the love of power to the power of love?" In many parts of the world, the church, Christian faith, and political power are no longer unified. The church's mission can no longer be the expansion of the "Christian" world.

In many places the church is a minority without privilege or access to power. Fortunately the church has been liberated from some of the power involvements that made it a burden on society rather than a servant. It has had to practice the faith in creative ways. Loss of power can thus be a blessing to the church. Not every loss of church privilege is anti-Christian. After the Ethiopian Orthodox Church lost power in the 1974 revolution, it was forced to reevaluate its task.

Ideologies can make the church aware of the human desire for equality and justice. Too often, though, Christians demonstrate unbiblical values in daily life—sensual pleasure, luxury, excessive wealth, enormous profit, competition, and consumerism. Faith degenerates into cheap grace with a health-and-wealth gospel. Jesus' example of servanthood and suffering is lost. An ideology like Marxism challenges the church to liberation and justice in the face of such perversions.

Ideologies can show us how indifferent we are to human need. Can we learn from their ability to evoke self-sacrifice and passionate devotion? I remember the passion of the Ethiopian Revolution in seeking to deal decisively with illiteracy, health care, and agricultural reform. It was a passion similar to religious conviction. Sometimes Marxists claim objectives that Christians consider as their own. Can we recover a social conscience, marked by compassion and Christian morality? Can we come to grips with the evils of social systems? To do so, we need a broader definition of the spiritual, a more holistic theology. Regret for our power alliances in the past should not make us politically irrelevant. We do not promote a private piety that withdraws from social involvement. Neither do we take all our cues from the ideology; we do not want to be taken over by it.

Ideologies can help the church regain its prophetic role. The church must nurture the prophetic elements of its own spirituality from the impulses of the Old and New Testaments. Frequently the church has been too preoccupied with correct dogma, individualistic Christianity, church structures, and denominational programs. Can we accept, for example, the Marxist criticism of religion as a clue for the renewal of the church? Are we willing to be prophetic in our criticism of religion? Did not the prophets and Jesus criticize religion? After all, Jesus criticized the Pharisees and Sadducees.

We agree that religion can become superstitious, magical, or a projection of human thought. We acknowledge that religion can become an alienating factor in human life. It can also become an opiate or drug to quiet uneasiness over that alienation. But we dare not accept that religion is nothing more than this.

*Ideologies Develop as a Result of Religion*

Some ideologies are a direct result of religious teaching. Religion has played a role in the development of capitalism. Apartheid developed as a "Christian heresy" based upon the Bible. Ideologies can result from the church's failure in teaching and practice.

Abuse of religion has caused some ideologies to become antireligious. Marx was responding to the abuse of religion. He attacked religion for its many faults, yet the categories of Marxist thought are quite religious. Marxism has succeeded in societies where churches were allied with power

against the disadvantaged, such as in the Soviet Union and
Ethiopia.

## The Church Is Conditioned by Ideology

All of us live with ideology; we cannot avoid ideological
influences. Yet it is easy to be molded by the dominant ideology. People act according to their interests or socioeconomic preferences rather than in accord with biblical
values. Churches and theologies frequently reinforce prevailing ideologies. For example, in the United States, evan-
gelicals involved in politics have supported the existing
political-economic establishment.

We must resist seduction by such cultural Christianity.
The church must analyze and criticize its own bias and self-
interest so as not to perpetuate the ideology of its culture.
The gospel loses its meaning when it is too closely associated with ideology. Gandhi was attracted to Jesus but
repelled by a church which practiced apartheid. The
Vietnamese had difficulty understanding the gospel in an
American ideology. The church takes human form in a
particular cultural-ideological situation; yet it must never
be bound by it. It always stretches across the boundaries of
culture and ideology. We will never be free from their influence, but we must join the struggle.

Sometimes ideology influences biblical interpretation
and theology. Theological statements are marked by time
and place. There are ideological elements in sermons. Doctrines have been put to ideological use. Church teachings
and practices have—consciously or not—supported the established order. For example, in one ideological situation,
the poor may be taught to be patient. In another situation,
the poor are taught to liberate themselves. Differing classes

of people interpret Jesus differently. The poor in Latin America interpret the Bible differently from the rich. The whites in South Africa have one interpretation, and the blacks another. Theology thus becomes the tool of ideology. Theology is not always determined by ideology nor can theology be reduced to ideology.

We become most conscious of our beliefs when we meet believers with differing interpretations. Often such differences result from differences in ideology rather than theology. We become aware of our own ideology through the mirror of another's ideology. Of course, it is much easier to recognize another's ideology than our own. It is helpful to look at our ideological understandings through the eyes of those hurt by our ideology.

*God's Providence and Ideology*

Joseph Horomadka of Czechoslovakia spoke of the judgment of God on the unfaithful who sought power instead of faithfulness. Was Marxism a judgment upon the failure of nineteenth-century Christians in Europe? The church then was captive to the power structures of the world. It had created an alien god who supported unjust systems. Marxist accusations were against specific Christian moral failures. Can ideology be part of God's judgment upon the church (see Isaiah 10)? Could God use Marxists to judge an unjust society and open the church's eyes to a concern for justice?

I believe God "wrestles with the world," and expresses his providence in judgment and in grace. God uses unbelievers to achieve his purposes in history. Assyria was an instrument of judgment upon Israel, the "rod of God's anger." Persia, under Cyrus (God's anointed), was an instrument of liberation. But if ideologies are instruments of judgment, they are also under judgment. (Note, for instance, the destruction of Assyria.)

A word of caution is needed here. In the 1960s some Christians were euphoric about the changes happening in China. They saw it as God's salvation in history outside the church. The task of the church was to cooperate with God. China equaled God's kingdom because justice was done: the oppressed were liberated and the broken healed.

As it turned out, this was much too naive. God's activity is never exhausted by what he does by secular means. God's providence is not necessarily salvation. Justice is not full salvation. It is idolatrous to identify God's salvation with any particular human movement.

If it was wrong to overidealize the Chinese Revolution it was equally wrong to reject totally its value. Some saw it as atheistic and, therefore, the embodiment of evil—the work of the devil. Belief in God's guidance and care enables us to be more objective. We can see destructive and constructive elements, but that does not diminish the importance of God's salvation. The church as an organized body had difficulty surviving, but its survival and growth is a work of grace. The church, too, has experienced liberation. It is working for greater justice, peace, simplicity, and morality.

Yet the remaining social and economic inequalities in Chinese society leave people searching for meaning. One can find full salvation only in God's work of grace in Jesus Christ. And to this the church gives witness.

CHAPTER 5

# A Biblical
# Perspective
# on Ideologies

We have noted how one can use ideology as a system of thought to interpret history and society, either to defend or to change existing social structures. Now we will examine the Old and New Testaments for clues that might provide a biblical perspective. Although concern for ideology is a recent development, I believe the Bible shows how faith can stand amid specific systems that are at once religious, political, social, and economic.

*Old Testament*

In Genesis 11, God brought judgment upon a self-centered social system at Babel. In Genesis 12, God called Abraham to leave Ur of the Chaldeans, a highly developed but wicked civilization, to go on pilgrimage. God would make a covenant with Abraham. On the way, Lot was seduced by Sodom. Had Abraham not interceded for Lot, he would have lost his soul and his life in the judgment brought upon Sodom (Genesis 18, 19).

Egypt had an ideology foreign to Israel. There were many gods there, and Pharaoh himself was deified. Abraham was the first to discover Egypt's power. Years later, Joseph was sold to Egypt. Joseph adjusted to the culture of Egypt, adopting Egyptian customs. In the face of temptation, he refused to compromise his moral integrity—even in suffering.

Oppression in Egypt increased. Later, Moses was saved from death and was reared in Pharaoh's court (Exodus 2). Nevertheless, Moses rejected Egyptian ideology and took the side of his people, the Hebrews. Concerned for justice, Moses killed an Egyptian (Exodus 2:11-12), apparently hoping to spark a movement for liberation (Acts 7:23-25). For this, Moses became a political refugee in Midian. Later God called Moses and used him to liberate the Hebrews from this ungodly ideology.

After a long pilgrimage through the Sinai desert, Israel entered Canaan. The Canaanites, known for their cultural achievements, shared an ideology held together by Canaanite religion. God warned Israel against this Canaanite idolatry (Deuteronomy 12:32—13:18). We learn that Israel's skirmishes with the Canaanites went in cycles (see Judges). Israel's sin of idolatry met with renewed oppression from the enemy until Israel repented and God again delivered them. The cycle then repeated itself. Even though God opposed Canaanite ideology, Israel borrowed ideas to guarantee her success. This foreign ideology plagued Israel long after she had become a nation. Instead of providing success, it became the root of injustice and exploitation.

Soon, Israel wanted a king, a dynasty, a human institution. God knew Israel would want to copy other nations, including those of the Near East. Here the king was a viceroy for God, while in Egypt he was worshiped as a god. Eventually, God let them have a king, but a prophet was to advise the king. Before long, Saul and David, taking their cues from other ideological understandings, acted unwisely and were rebuked by prophets.

Under Solomon, Israel reached its greatest outward splendor. It also began its period of decline. Israel developed commercially, industrially, and culturally. But this development led to oppression instead of justice. Solomon lived more and more like an Oriental despot and forgot the wisdom of his earlier years. He accepted alien influence and gradually moved into idolatry. Idolatry had a greater effect on the future than all the economic and cultural splendor. Solomon's tolerance embraced ideologies foreign to the character of Israel. God did not call Israel to be a "great nation," but a "separate nation." Following Solomon, the kingdom divided into two—Israel and Judah.

The issue now was no longer only the foreign ideologies—Babel, Ur, Sodom, Egypt, and the Canaanites. Israel and Judah struggled with the problem of *their own* ideology. Following Solomon's example, foreign religions and ideologies entered the kingdoms with their own religious ideologies. Against this mixture of ideologies (syncretism) the prophets struggled. The problem now was no longer just "their" ideology, but "our ideology."

Where had the ideology of Israel and Judah gone wrong? The basic problem was that the rise of kingship threatened the rule of God. Israel and Judah never came to give divine honor to the king as their neighbors did, but God was no longer their sole king.

Citizenship in a state replaced covenant loyalty to God.

The covenant strictly forbade such mixed loyalty, requiring absolute devotion to the will of God. (See Deuteronomy 5.)

Ideology functioned within Israel and Judah as a civil religion—a religion used for social and political purposes (Amaziah, Ahaz, Manasseh). Forms, ceremonies, and sacrifices flourished, but holiness, mercy, and justice withered. Civil religion expressed itself in the temple-military complex within Judah.

The prophets addressed issues of idolatry, politics, economics, land, administration of justice, power, and pride. They emphasized that God was the judge of every social order. They said that if Israel and Judah lost their distinctive faith in God, the ideologies of the Near East would swallow them up. God remained above and beyond Hebrew society and politics as he remained above and beyond foreign systems. If God's people became like other nations, he would no longer deliver them *from* their enemies but *to* their enemies. By judging the ideologies of Egypt and the Canaanites, God delivered Israel and Judah.

Through disobedience, however, Israel's and Judah's own ideologies were now subject to judgment. God could use even Assyria, Babylon, and Persia to accomplish his purpose in judgment. (See Isaiah 10:5-7, Jeremiah 25:9, and Isaiah 45:1.) Israel fell to Assyria in 722 B.C. and Judah to Babylon in 587 B.C.

The story of Daniel and his friends in Babylon helps us to face a revolutionary situation (Daniel 1-6). In the first place, they were willing to *cooperate*. They served in the palace, were educated in Babylonian culture and language, and received new names. But cooperation was not total submission, nor blind approval. They asked to be excused from certain kinds of food and drink, since people associated these with idols. Their objections, however, were not just negative. They understood the culture well enough to propose alternatives. Discernment enabled them to maintain their integrity.

In the second place, Daniel and his friends provided *prophetic interpretation* of this ideology. Daniel interpreted Nebuchadnezzar's dreams when the local magicians, enchanters, and sorcerers failed. Daniel interpreted the handwriting on the wall for King Belshazzar. After much prayer and counsel with his friends, Daniel provided an answer to the king. Daniel was in tune with a power the magicians did not have. Though his predictions were harsh, he did not give them in a spirit of pride or condemnation. Babylonian culture (ideology) would not endure.

In the third place, Daniel and his friends *resisted* the ideology. They refused to bow down to the golden image. Babylonian divinities and images were associated with the kingdom. Any refusal to worship them was considered a failure in patriotism. Daniel's friends, however, passionately resisted a despot bent on taking away their freedom to worship God. For this refusal, they were thrown into a furnace.

Daniel lived to see his adopted kingdom (Babylon) replaced by Persia (Daniel 6). Again Daniel was discerning and cooperative. Because of his fine spirit, he became secretary-treasurer in the kingdom. But he would not give up his practice of praying toward Jerusalem. He considered the worship of God more important than the law of the Medes and Persians. He put faith before ideology. For his refusal to compromise, he was thrown into a den of lions.

Esther's relationship to the Persian Empire was similar to Daniel's. She was willing to serve as queen, but she risked her good name and her life to stop the evil plans to kill her people. She, too, both cooperated with and resisted the ideology of her time.

*New Testament*

In the Gospels, both Jesus (Luke 4:43; Mark 1:14-15) and John the Baptist (Matthew 3:1-12) proclaimed the kingdom of God. The kingdom of God was a present reality in the person, action, and word of Jesus. Jesus' followers continued the ministry of announcing that kingdom (Luke 9:1-2; 10:9). The kingdom became the judge of all other systems. John the Baptist's allegiance to the kingdom enabled him to criticize Herod and earned him a place in prison (Luke 3:19-20). Jesus, in temptations at the beginning of his ministry, refused all other kingdoms (Matthew 4:1-11). The dominant Roman ideology of Jesus' day spawned Jewish ideologies. These sought to define a Jewish relationship with Rome. Jesus encountered both Roman and Jewish ideologies, but he did not choose the particular ideology of any one Jewish group.

The Essenes were ascetics who withdrew from political turmoil to the desert beside the Dead Sea. They were waiting for God to overthrow the powers of evil and inaugurate a new kingdom.

The Pharisees also expected God to intervene, and so they were passive to Roman rule. They expressed their main concern for personal and group piety within their own community in detailed religious observance.

The Sadducees related to both the religious and political power groups. Noted for their tolerance and compromise, they yielded power to Rome so long as temple activities could continue. They tried to be responsible in meeting social needs by working with the Romans. They could make little change, however, because they were too closely identified with the ruling power.

The Herodians also worked with the Romans and supported their programs. As a small, privileged upper class, they profited from cooperation with the oppressors.

The problem with the Essenes, Pharisees, Sadducees, and Herodians is that none of them did much to challenge the existing power. In fact, their inaction tended to reinforce the existing secular power.

The Zealots were revolutionaries of the "left." They were the loyalists, the freedom fighters against the Roman military establishment. They believed they could begin the kingdom of God through their own efforts, so they developed a system of counterforce and violence.

The Zealots resemble the Maccabeans who revolted against their Hellenistic oppressors (Seleucids). Both are examples of revolutionary ideology. Their goals were understandable; they wanted justice. Their religious motivation was strong. The Maccabees succeeded, the Zealots did not.

Jesus rejected all of these ideological options. He was guided by God's kingdom values. He did not support the establishment Jews nor the crusading revolutionary Jews. The establishment had the temple, the priesthood, the Scriptures, and religious learning. They stood for law and order. The revolutionaries were concerned for righteousness and justice. Jesus did not choose one or the other. Jesus knew that revolution or establishment were both inadequate.

By not siding with those who were for or against Rome he could appeal to Romans and Jews. He had a message for the centurion, the Zealot, and the tax collector. He could address all because his identity was in God's kingdom, a new power center. This prevented him from identifying with or blessing any one ideology. Jesus' teaching about God's kingdom undermined the values of ideology. Jesus had compassion for the victims of ideology. Injustice and exploitation were wrong wherever they appeared. He threatened the power balance between the Romans and the Jews by confronting the power groups in his society— intellectual, economic, political, religious. He called Herod a fox. He threatened the privileged Sadducees. He criticized the legal experts for placing burdens upon people, the rich for refusing to share their wealth, and the rulers for abusing their power.

Jesus was not a slave of any power, law, custom, institution, or ideological theory. One could live under Caesar, but Caesar did not have ultimate authority (Mark 12:17). Although Jesus subjected himself to Roman and Jewish power, he refused to allow them to control him. This led him into conflict with the Jewish Sanhedrin and the Roman governor. Finally, the high priest, Caiaphas, and Pilate, the Roman governor, turned against him. Jewish power and Roman power acted together to crucify him.

The early church understood that God's kingdom was in tension with other powers. When Peter and John were tried before the Sanhedrin they replied, "We must obey God, not men" (Acts 5:29). The *religious* establishment put Stephen to death (Acts 6—8) and moved against the Christians (Acts 9:1-2). *Philosophical* systems were challenged by the gospel (Acts 17).

*Political* power was also threatened, so Herod had James put to death (Acts 12:1-3). Because the Jews did not want to disturb relations with Rome, they sought to gain Roman favor by accusing Christians. They accused Paul and Silas of "breaking the laws of the Emperor, saying that there is another king, whose name is Jesus" (Acts 17:7). While Paul was critical of Rome, he could also claim his rights as a Roman citizen under Roman law (Acts 21:39).

The gospel also undermined *economic* interests. At Philippi, Paul and Silas caused people to lose money by healing a girl that had a spirit of divination. The accusation was "they are causing trouble in our city. They are teaching customs that are against our law" (Acts 16:16-24). At Ephesus Paul ruined the economy when believers left their idolatry and no longer purchased silver shrines of the goddess Artemis (Acts 19:23-41).

These examples show that the kingdom of God came before all other powers, whether religious, philosophical, political, or economic. The New Testament declares that Christ is above all powers (Colossians 1:15-19). All principalities and powers are under his control (1 Corinthians 15:24; Ephesians 1:21-23). Believers need not fear these powers (Romans 8:38). Rather, the church is to witness to them (Ephesians 3:11). A Christian gives absolute allegiance to no prince or principle but to Jesus alone.

According to Romans 12:14—13:8 we live with the powers and we cooperate to the extent possible. We recognize the importance of social order and acknowledge that God's providence can be expressed through such order. We do not blindly submit, however, or bow down to the powers. As John H. Yoder suggests (see his *Politics of Jesus*), we practice a kind of "revolutionary subordination." This is neither full approval of power nor fanatic resistance against power. We are subject within limits. Where ideologies point away from God or take the place of God, we resist. Romans 13 applies to all ideologies—those that seek to displace the church and those that seek to use the church.

The early church was a movement of God into the public life of the world claiming the allegiance of *all* persons. The Old Testament confessed "Yahweh is God" and challenged other competing systems. The New Testament claim that "Jesus is Lord" puts the church on a collision course with established powers and alien ideologies.

*Summary of Biblical Perspectives*

The Bible reflects many different situations and ideologies which affected how early believers expressed their faith. From these biblical examples, we learn that the church must always test ideologies by the will of God. Ideologies can reject God, distort God, ignore God, or replace God. When an ideology points away from God, believers must correct or resist the ideology, for God's kingdom is supreme.

Since ideologies often combine several elements, we need to test them to see what is good or bad. At times it is possible to be subject to, to cooperate with, to serve within, and to make room for particular functions of the ideology. Yet we need careful discernment if we are not to be conditioned by it. Such discernment is more important than "blanket approval" or "blanket rejection." The believing community is too easily influenced by ideology. It is not enough to select one of the current ideological options. The genius of the church is to see other choices.

Ideologies are often in conflict with each other. Some seek to maintain society as it is (establishment). Others seek

to change society (revolutionary). These are sometimes
called "rightist" or "leftist" positions. Jesus' life suggests
that it is not enough to be establishment or revolutionary.
The truth must address both systems.

While the church does not ally itself with any one
ideology, it dare not use this as an excuse to withdraw from
social responsibility. When the church teaches and lives
kingdom values, its social actions will challenge ideologies.
Some of these values may even be similar to the values of a
particular ideology, yet no ideology fully represents kingdom values. Thus the church must be faithful to the
kingdom vision rather than making alliances with any one
ideology.

# CHAPTER 6

# *Faith Judges*
# *All Ideologies*

*The Kingdom Perspective*

The kingdom of God revealed in Jesus judges all ideologies. The kingdom rises above ideologies because its goals lie beyond ideology. It cannot be equated with any political, economic, or social system. It crowds them out of first place. The Lord of the church is greater than all other lords. As part of God's kingdom, the church serves as a positive force in the kingdom systems of the world.

The kingdom does not give us a particular political theory or specific tools for political analysis. It does, however, raise questions and provide answers for the most important concerns in life. The values of God's kingdom affect the way we analyze the past and present, work for change, or project the future. Kingdom values will prevent us from harming others in order to help them. We know that turning human systems into a god destroys people. We must allow God to be God if humans are to be humans.

We do not critique ideologies by comparing them to each other. Rather, we evaluate them in the light of Christian faith and God's kingdom. Ideologies force us to return

to Scripture. We must insist on a biblical critique of
ideologies. The Word of God must not lose its supreme authority. In the midst of the ideological struggle in South
Africa, Beyers Naude wrote the following.

> If the Word of God is not the fire that renews us, other fires
> shall devour us; if the Word of God is not the hammer that
> crushes rocks, other hammers shall destroy us. (Allan
> Boesak, *Farewell to Innocence*)

When we give full allegiance to the kingdom of God, all
other loyalties take a lesser place. While some choices are
better than others, one choice is absolute: Who will be
God? When we turn something relative into an absolute (a
god), we become idolaters.

The kingdom of God is universal and therefore international. Christians are first of all world citizens. All of our
loyalties are secondary to God's kingdom. Christians must,
therefore, promote the command of God, not a particular
ideology. We speak of brothers and sisters rather than capitalists or socialists. We must resist interpreting Christian
faith through one specific ideology. How tragic it is when
the gospel is too closely identified with a specific culture,
form of politics, moral system, or ideology. We know that
Christianity has frequently fallen into this trap. God is not a
tribal god, for God remains above all national, racial, and
cultural barriers.

Sometimes faith has functioned as an ideology, but this
is not its role. We do not uphold faith as a new form of
ideology but as an opportunity for a new relationship in the
kingdom. From this perspective we evaluate all ideologies.
Christians can then work in situations that are not to their

liking with whatever freedoms they have. If the church is truly universal, it can exist in any ideological environment. We acknowledge that all systems contain some truth and falsehood. We do not reject truth because it is spoken by an ideological enemy, for it does not therefore cease to be the truth. Neither do we foolishly champion one ideological system over another.

## Ideologies Become Absolutist and Idolatrous

Christians dare never grant ideologies the importance their advocates claim for them. Such persons or groups present their ideologies as the only reality, as absolute truth for all people, requiring total allegiance. Such claims lead either to sneering disbelief or excessive zeal. Some of us cannot forget the arrogance and fanaticism of Nazism as totalitarian systems compete with and distort the gospel. Total Christian commitment therefore threatens such systems.

Christians challenge ideology because kingdom citizens owe an undivided loyalty to Christ. The people of God reject false claims of authority and dominion (nationalism, capitalism, Marxism) believing that absolute truth comes only from God. Christian faith restrains ideologies from the tendency to make partial truths absolute. All claims of an absolute system eventually fracture humans and lead to a fractured society. Ideologies claim to do good but resort to evil. Those seeking for change become the new instrument for opposing change.

Ideologies have a tendency to "play God." They set themselves up as idols. The Christian's duty is to examine them critically. For example, capitalism expresses a subtle idolatry when it exploits others and ignores God, as Marxism does when it denies God. Apartheid, when it blesses Afrikaner nationalism and disregards God's standards of justice, becomes an idol. When national security states or the Iranian Revolution demand unquestioning obedience, they serve as idols. God wishes to dethrone such idols. Biblical faith does not oppose ideologies, but it does idols. Faith must reject the idolatry within an ideology. The cross brings judgment upon every ideology that claims first place in our lives. Christ has defeated these principalities and powers.

## Ideologies as Religion

Ideologies easily turn themselves into religion. Sometimes the religious dimensions of ideology make it difficult to see clearly the difference between religion and ideology. Ideology looks like religious faith because, like faith, it makes meaning and value statements about human nature, society, and history. It also demands the total commitment of followers to realize the vision. The ideology is embraced with self-sacrifice and passionate, religious-like devotion. Ideologies function as religion when they offer doctrines of salvation or rituals that take the place of the church and sacraments. Because of their similarity to religion, ideologies can question faith, compete with faith, repress faith, or replace faith. By distorting faith they offer deceptive grounds for hope.

Marxism, because of parallels with Christianity, seems to be a secularized version of the kingdom of God. Marx was not really able to escape the thought of the Bible. He seems to have believed in the kingdom of God without God. Marx developed a kind of Scripture, doctrine, ethics, understanding of the future, an elite group, and a mission.

Marxism has sacred times, sacred places, sacred words, sacred persons. Like religion, it is authoritarian and considers itself infallible.

*Discerning Ideologies*

Though ideologies can become idols or function as religion, we should not quickly call an ideology demonic. Ideologies are not of the devil; they are human creations. However, since humans are sinful, aspects of ideologies can become demonic. Ideologies are seductive, not because they are all bad, but because bad and good mix in them. It is not helpful to say "capitalism is bad" or "socialism is good," or the reverse. It is equally unhelpful to consider the American Revolution "of God" and the Russian Revolution "not of God." Oppression or justice do not belong to one ideology alone; sin or righteousness is not the exclusive property of one or the other.

More careful discernment is required to understand and analyze wisely. Only when we understand can we recognize limits and counter the false claims of ideologies. Correct information is basic. Ignorance, worn-out slogans, overstatements, or false information confuse the issue. For instance, not all movements for social liberation are Marxist. Knowledge and sound judgment go before challenge.

We must evaluate ideologies on several levels. What do they say? What do they mean? For example, what does freedom of religion mean? How does theory come together in practice? What are the goals? What is the motivation behind the goals? We might agree with basic ideas but find the underlying philosophy objectionable. Or we might agree with goals but reject the means to achieve them.

Does the ideology represent reality fairly or distort it? Are humans valued as whole persons? Is there place for that which lies beyond human experience? What is the attitude toward the church? Does the ideology only conserve the past, or does it have a vision for the future? Does it work for the good of the majority, or favor one sex, race, or class?

A key issue lies in the relationship of ideology and power. The church must be alert, not simply to ideas but to the use of power. There is legitimate use of power but also abuse of power. The quest for power, security, and self-interest often includes many evils.

Sometimes ideologies can be evaluated positively—they perform necessary functions. They are useful tools. They symbolize collective good. They express parts of Christian social commitment. At other times, ideologies function negatively—they distort or repress facts. They reject the transcendent. They sacrifice human dignity, creativity, and freedom. It is not enough to see only the positive or the negative side. Our evaluation of ideologies must be fair, precise, sensitive, and free. We must test ideology point by point, and not as an inseparable whole. Only then can we see the points of agreement or disagreement with Christian values.

*Strengths and Weaknesses of Ideologies*

Following the 1974 Revolution in Ethiopia, I used *Communist Faith and Christian Faith* by Donald Evans as a resource in educational settings. My approach, taken from the book, considered several issues and asked: What do communists believe? What do Christians believe? Where do we agree? Where do we disagree? What are the Christian options? This issue-by-issue approach proved helpful. It must replace uncritical name-calling or stereo-typing. It forces us to choose between ideology and biblical principles and not between ideologies. Further, we do not feel obliged to accept or reject the whole ideology. Looked at this way, we will find agreement and disagreement at specific points between ideologies and faith.

Christians agree with Marxists when they call for social responsibility, economic equality, and human rights to end injustice. Christians value the concern for human welfare. They, too, want more social freedom within community and agree that individual freedom often degenerates into selfish freedom that exploits others. They admit that the power of economic interests and the idolatry of money cause alienation.

Christians accept the importance of history, a vision for the future, and the need for social change. Action is better than speculation. They admit that the Marxist criticism of religion is partly right. Christians have often defended God while neglecting the cries of the oppressed. Religion has it-self sometimes been a cause of alienation. Much of what Marxists say about the political side of religious ideas and institutions is true. People have used religion to conserve and defend unjust social structures and to prevent op-pressed people from seeing their need for social change. The Marxist critique helps the church to purge itself of alien additions to the biblical message and to recover the prophetic content of its faith.

However, Christians also disagree with Marxists. In general, the similarities between Christians and Marxists relate to social ideals. The conflicts are caused by different understandings of meaning, human nature, and the meth-ods for achieving the goals. Marxism is better at criticizing other systems than at giving answers. Christians appreciate certain insights but are skeptical of Marxism as an ideology. Christians have difficulty with the emphasis on material, rather than spiritual things. They reject the notion that human society can be perfected, that God does not exist, and that economics determines history.

Though history is important in Marxism, God does not figure in the historical process. Human alienation is real but it is deeper than Marx imagined. The problem of alienation from God requires a more radical remedy than the restructuring of society. Failure to recognize sin leads to too much confidence in human beings, for evil is considered to depend upon the economic system.

Does elimination of private property really change human behavior? Are humans changed through social engineering? The fatal flaw in Marxism is its limited view of humans. The Bible teaches that we are not fully human except in relation to the Creator. Human ideals do not depend solely on social and economic causes. Humans are not the center of history, nor can they perfect the world. Humans need God.

Christians reject the antireligious bias of Marxism. Marx did not understand Jesus and the prophetic tradition of the Bible. Biblical faith is not a narcotic for the oppressed. The prophets and Jesus made the oppressors uncomfortable; they did not side with the authorities against the poor. Biblical teaching causes change in social conditions. Christians were first agents for change, not defenders of unjust systems. Marx was right in seeing that religion *can be* an opiate, but wrong in thinking it *has to be* or is by nature. (Even Marx said religion was not always opium.) He was also wrong when he predicted the demise of religion. Marxism fails where capitalism fails: by trusting in the material. In fact, Marxism easily becomes the opiate it denounces. For Marxism asks the person who is suffering now to sacrifice the present for the dream of the future.

Christians object to the totalitarian tendencies of Marxism. This includes propaganda and pressure on those who dare to differ, thereby limiting freedom. When people are deprived of freedom they lose some of their human dignity. In the process of seeking liberation, people are also dehumanized. Christians are critical of class struggle, violent revolution, and selective ethics. Christians critique Marxists who reject compassion, because it may preserve a present system and delay the arrival of a new one.

Many Christians have supported democratic capitalism because of its ideals of equality and freedom. Liberal democracies emphasize equality before the law, as well as equality of dignity, opportunity, and responsibility. They speak of freedom from fear, freedom of speech, freedom of association, and freedom of religion. They encourage the development of individual potential. Voluntary participation is considered the lifeblood of a free society. Discussion and consent are to characterize human relations. The state is a mechanism to achieve ends higher than itself. Only if the people are more important than the state can one avoid state control. Many of these values appear to converge with Christian understandings of human freedom and dignity. But Christians are becoming more aware of failures in equality and freedom brought about by the marriage of democracy and capitalism.

Christians must criticize the gap between the affluent and the desperately poor, the large sums spent on military and luxury goods, the growing power of giant multinational corporations. They must condemn the capitalist domination of the state, the growing power of the military and related industries, and the alliance of capitalism with imperialism.

When the free market system, profit, and the accumulation of capital come first, problems arise. People hoard resources. Alienation, waste, consumerism, gluttony, inequality, and injustice abound. Capital, technology, and marketing have an underside: unemployment, poverty, dehumanization. People soon become things manipulated for economic purposes. Capitalism at its worst maximizes economic gain, stimulates grasping, idealizes the strong, and subordinates people to economic production.

Can selfishly motivated individuals create social good? Does the capitalist system serve the people or the people serve the system? Does the system respect the dignity of all persons and promote the common good? Does the system encourage concern for others or selfishness? We must therefore ask if the ideology behind liberal democratic capitalism is in harmony with the gospel. Christians must criticize the basic assumptions of the liberal mind—the progressive view of history, the radical freedom of individuals, and the piling up of wealth as a primary goal. Liberal democratic capitalism cannot provide the solution to alienation and loneliness. Liberals do not understand fallenness and sin. Accumulation of wealth does not free.

Humanity is only free in a covenant relationship. Christians need to break radically with capitalism at significant points. They have compromised with the ideology too long.

This brief look at Marxism and capitalism should convince us that we dare not allow any ideological system to hold us captive. From a Christian perspective, all ideological systems are flawed, for they tend to exploit us. The world views of both Marxism and liberal capitalism are preoccupied with economics. Each sees human freedom as the final goal as though persons without economic needs were free. The power of Marxism and capitalism needs limits, especially when ideology is embodied in the Marxist and capitalist superpowers. A joke in Eastern Europe says, "Under capitalism man exploits man; under communism it's the other way around."

In the practice of Marxism and capitalism, a gap exists between goals and reality. Ans J. van der Bent (*Christians and Communists*, page 32) says, "Christianity in the West betrays Christ by accommodating itself to the status quo, while the U.S.S.R. betrays Marx by becoming just another bourgeois power." Christians totally reject the atheism of Marxism but ask whether atheism is essential to Marxism. Some argue that one can accept Marxism without atheism as some in India have done. Others believe it dangerously easy to underestimate its permeating impact. Yet ideologies other than Marxism are also atheistic. Alexander Solzhenitsyn reminds us that the West is morally and spiritually bankrupt.

When we examine ideology point by point we feel some agreement with certain goals. The church may discover itself on the same side on some issues. We can affirm our agreements without affirming unity. But we must pay careful attention to the relationship. We do not want to "Marxize" Christianity or "Christianize" Marxism. We strongly object to "Christianizing" capitalism or "capitalizing" Christianity. We must evaluate both Marxism and capitalism by the standard of God's kingdom values.

Real liberation cannot come if we lock ourselves into these two choices. Because the church transcends all ideologies, it is free to affirm and to reject aspects of each. We identify good and evil, truth and falsehood. We are for political and religious liberty and we are for peace and justice. We insist on being biblically faithful, not captive to an ideology.

## Faith Not Ideology

Faith is a response to a call from outside the society. Faith and ideology are therefore not on the same level of knowledge and action. But they are not necessarily opposed to each other; they are two different spheres. When faith becomes merely a "Christian ideology," the collective guiding beliefs of a human group, it loses its unique quality, its universality, and its promise. It then becomes a Christian civilization which replaces the kingdom. (See Andre Dumas here.)

Christian faith is superior to all ideologies. It is able to see the good and bad in each. It supports aspects informed by Christian insights or those that help people struggle for justice. It encourages ideology in drawing out human potential and criticizes it for undermining such potential. Faith uncovers blindness associated with ideology, whether innocent or willful. Sin lurks behind even our best intentions.

But faith goes one step farther. It contributes insights not contained in the ideology. There is another vision. It is the kingdom vision, a vision for change and hope.

# CHAPTER 7

# Developing a Stance Toward Ideologies

When we critique ideologies from the perspective of God's kingdom we question the total claims of these systems. At the same time, however, we acknowledge the role of ideologies in society. They are a means to some ends but not ends in themselves. When possible we work for tolerance and mutual understanding. As strangers and pilgrims we are at home anywhere but alien everywhere. We live then in the tension between rejection and assimilation. We look for a choice between opposition to, or embrace of ideology.

### Spirit of Objection

Prior allegiance to God's kingdom is no excuse for a spirit of arrogance. We examine aspects of ideology with an open mind. Let us be fair in our interpretation of a specific ideology. Christians frequently concentrate on the negative, such as the persecution of Christians by Marxists or oppression of the poor by capitalists. Though the ideology spreads ideas or rumors to help itself or to hinder another ideology, such propaganda is not the method for us. Words and expressions such as *communist, capitalist, iron curtain, and bourgeois* can mold attitudes and trap us in negative thinking. Let us be careful in our use of language, for words have the power to open or close our minds.

Our job is not to fight the ideological battle but to represent the Christian message. If we fight evil on its own terms, we become like the evil we oppose. There is, of course, the danger of seduction, but our response should not be to attack or condemn. We are loving adversaries. Hostility arises from fear. It expresses itself in worn-out slogans and expressions. It leads to crusades of anticommunism or anticapitalism. If we merely take an "anti" stance, we have oversimplified the conflict and clouded the real issues. Religious propaganda can be as destructive as antireligious propaganda. Hostility produces counterideology. Faith then degenerates into an ideology.

We do not need to either justify ideologies or condemn them, but we do need to deprive them of their significance. Discernment is needed if we are not to be naive or gullible. This calls for criticism, confrontation, and sometimes even resistance. But we are not just *against something, we are for* something; we are proactive, not just reactive. We have a "responsible" attitude.

### Avoid Extreme Positions

When a revolution changes the existing ideology, the church may feel guilt for having reacted against the change. At such times, it is easy to treat the new ideology as heroic and too hastily bless it. I have a friend who in the midst of revolution thanked God that the day had come for which they had prayed. Several months later he, along with others, was disappointed. It is right to divorce ourselves from earlier unholy alliances with ideology but we should not too quickly accept another. In one third-world country, I saw people rush out to purchase Mao's *Red Book* from street vendors. Later, however, this optimism turned to pessimism. To describe the Chinese Revolution as "birth pangs of the kingdom," as some scholars did, was misleading because it was premature.

It is easier to look back and see how the church compromised with ideologies than to be alert to our compromises today. It is absolutely wrong for the church in South Africa to ally itself with apartheid. It is equally unwise for the church to accept blindly any ideology that opposes racial segregation. We reject unquestioning alliances with any power—the former or the new.

Earlier we noted that Jesus addressed both the establishment and the revolutionary. His example suggests a position above or between. He did not bless one nor oppose the other. Sometimes believers are like conservatives (e.g., against abortion on demand) and sometimes more like revolutionaries (e.g., opposition to nuclear armaments). Christians are free to examine both positions. Each may promote values that can be affirmed. Each may make outrageous claims that must be rejected. One ideology is not all good and the other all bad. Unfortunately, we sometimes allow our ideological bias to influence what we call sin or righteousness. Establishment types can be sinners; revolutionaries can be sinners. Defenders of the existing order may oppress, but revolutionaries can also oppress when they consolidate their power. We need to cultivate a realism that moves beyond ideology.

The real issue is whether we choose God, rather than the establishment or the revolution. When we choose God we can with integrity evaluate what is wrong or right in both. After such assessment, we may prefer one over the other, but we do not in principle declare one before another, without choosing God first. Christians in rightist situations may feel themselves close to the revolutionary left. If, on the other hand, Christians have experienced aspects of leftist radicalism, they may affirm some values of the establishment right. We seek to do God's will, but find that this is not exclusively on one side. Churches feel this tension because they are conservative and prophetic. The church's theology must come before ideology if it is to provide standards for ethical behavior and for criticizing ideologies of the right and left. God has chosen no favorite ideology, and neither do we.

This in-between position involves risk. We know it is not the task of the church to sanctify a specific ideology. How then can we be sure that God is for or against a particular political or social position of the ideology? It is even more confusing when Christians commit themselves to one faith, but endorse different ideologies. Since we cannot assume that our understanding is always the will of God, we must be modest. Yet we believe the church should promote an alternate way as a sign of the kingdom. So, guided by the values of Jesus, we participate in the society to contribute justly to it.

By this action, we do not seek to usher in the kingdom by programs based on some ideology. Any attempt to fuse Christianity with an ideology dilutes its character and prevents it from being a foretaste of the kingdom of heaven or the salt of the earth.

## A *Third Way*

After a revolution, two political parties were competing for power and persons were asked which side they were on. When Christians said they did not want to be wholly part of one or the other, they were suspect. Did Jesus take a neutral position? If we are neither establishment nor revolutionary, are we neutral? José Miguez Bonino says the church cannot be ideologically neutral. The *Kairos Document*, developed in South Africa by those who oppose apartheid, insists that the church not be a "third force" between the oppressed and the oppressor. Some liberation theologians say the church must take sides and support one ideology.

I have argued that the church finds itself above or between. It may not be "bought" by one side or the other. Without some distance, it is impossible to minister to everyone—the rich and the poor, the powerful and the powerless. However, we must also be careful that distance does not appear as a defense of the *status quo* or of the church's own interests.

I would suggest, however, that even though the church is beyond politics and ideologies, it has ethical concerns. These it brings to society, and believers take sides on specific issues. We are against oppression. We are not neutral about injustice. I opposed the United States bombing Hanoi. That did not compel me to endorse completely the North Vietnam regime. I am not a "flag waver" or a "flag burner."

The church cannot remain outside of political life. Even if the church is silent, it influences by inaction. We are obliged to speak and act with conviction for that which is right. But we are more free to do so if we have some independence from a particular ideology. Involvement on specific issues makes the church more effective rather than less because it focuses the nature of witness. I do not believe that one class holds a monopoly on moral rights or is closer to the kingdom. We defend the right and expose the wrong. That is more important than identifying completely with one class or one ideology. Expressing support on specific issues is not promoting the whole ideology.

## Ideologies Change

It is impossible to develop a stance toward ideologies that applies to all situations in which Christians live. Because of historical and cultural differences, it is difficult to make general statements about the position that the church should take. We should not concentrate only upon the ideology but upon the local expression of it. This is shaped by geography, economics, politics, foreign policy, culture, and the class structure of the society. Is the ideology in power or struggling for power? The longer the power struggle the more radical will be the expressions that emerge.

Are Marxism and Christianity compatible? Are capitalism and Christianity compatible? It depends upon how one defines Marxism. The dominant classical Marxism with an atheistic worldview is not compatible with Christianity. Parts of Marxist analysis and strategies for social change may be compatible. Socialist ideals of cooperation and sharing are compatible. Hans Kung said, "A Christian can be a socialist, but a Christian is not bound to be a socialist."

Just as one finds many kinds of Christians, one also finds many kinds of Marxists. Therefore, one cannot give a universal response about Marxisms and Marxists. For example, there is postrevolutionary Marxism of Eastern Europe and the Soviet Union. Marxism of the third world has its unique character. In Africa it is difficult for Marxism to remain atheistic.

Is Marxism a closed system or can it be self-critical? What kind of change is happening? Marxists and socialists change. Not all socialists advocate violent change. Ideologies sometimes become less idealistic and more practical. There may be moderation in the Marxist attitude toward religion. Or the church may invite change by mellowing its position toward ideology. The church's approach to each expression of Marxism will therefore differ.

As societies change over time, so ideologies crack, erode, and change. For example, China has become more tolerant of the church. Ideologies are not pure. Parts of Africa combine capitalism and socialism. We find some capitalism in the Soviet Union, Eastern Europe, and China. After resolving some of the problems of poverty, health, and hunger, socialist countries seek consumer goods. As ideologies change, Christians redefine their stance toward the ideology. This stance *may* differ from one place to another.

*Critical Participation*

I believe we can take both faith and ideology seriously. This critical participation includes a oneness with, but also a critical tension with, the ideology. I do not favor *withdrawal*, because it separates and makes enemies. It is not enough for Christians to be indifferent to the world. It is equally inadequate to *oppose* strongly the ideology, because we consider it totally evil. People become defensive when we take such a negative attitude.

It would likewise be foolish only to *conform* to or uncritically accept ideology. Too often the church has quickly identified with the prevailing ideology, ignoring or explaining away its injustices. Christians can easily be deceived. We remember what happened under Hitler. Only 10 percent of the pastors supported the confessing church, which opposed Nazi ideology. *Critical participation* rejects withdrawal, opposition, or conformity as adequate positions. It does incorporate aspects of them, depending upon the specific issue.

God's will cannot be equated with any ideology. Neither is there a specifically Christian socioeconomic analysis or plan of action. Therefore, the church will need to distinguish between how it prefers to work and what it considers necessary to carry out its purpose. Since one cannot divide the world into Christians and non-Christians, we have to work with the world, despite its conflicting ideologies. Can we accept our situation as an appointed place to bear witness to faith and hope? I believe we can if we are guided by critical participation.

This critical involvement allows us to hold ideological opinions in addition to our religious conviction. Since we do not live in a vacuum, ideology is necessary for society to function. Yet we are cautious and live in tension with it. We accept the world as God's good creation, aware that it is marked by sin.

While no social system is Christian, we can apply Christian values to an imperfect world. Ideologies are too optimistic and self-confident and eventually betray their goals to improve human life. They may have moral ideals but suffer from powerlessness. The church has a duty to correct, to warn about perversion, and to help ideologies become more human. The church recognizes that ideologies have both potential and limitations which merit support and judgment. It supports some of the goals of the ideology but punctures its false views of reality. It asks, what is God's will in history and what is not? What can the church support and what must it reject?

Our critical participation enables us to see that the kingdom of God makes all ideologies relative. We cannot take any of them with total seriousness. We act as prophets toward ideology. A Cuban suggested that one cannot be prophetic by remaining on the margin. Only when Christians have some involvement with the society can they function as critics.

We insist that the Christian worldview engage the worldview of specific ideologies. This calls for the church to clarify its identity but also to seriously interact with specific ideologies. Critical participation means the church will be attracted and repulsed by ideologies. If we join ideologies against injustice we also oppose them when they go astray. This calls for divine guidance and creative thinking as we combine spiritual discernment with practical judgment.

We live with the tension of loyalty and opposition, endorsement and criticism, knowledge and correction, subordination and resistance, acceptance and rejection, affirmation and judgment. Paul Mojzes says, "A Christian who can say "yes" to a society can meaningfully do so if she or he can also say "no.' " Does not the example of Jesus teach us to say yes and no?

## Is Cooperation with Ideology Possible?

When we take faith and ideology seriously we feel for Christians in other lands. For example, the Japanese Christian Kanzo Vchimura, appreciated "two J's—Jesus and Japan" and a Chinese Christian liked two C's—Christ and China. When there is critical participation, some cooperation is possible. Faith makes us free to criticize and cooperate.

Social concerns often form the common ground for the Christian to participate with the ideology. Christian expressions of social compassion are often similar to some of the goals of the ideology. Sometimes we work parallel with the ideology and sometimes we work together. If famine creates hunger in Ethiopia, we can cooperate with the system if necessary to provide famine relief. If China encourages the learning of English, we make English teachers available. The church can support efforts for justice, human rights, land reform, literacy, and health care. Common concern for social welfare does not mean that we have a common identity.

In China the state stripped the church of its buildings, denominational structures, budgets, hospitals, schools, orphanages, and social programs. As believers scattered throughout the secular structures, the gospel was diffused in Chinese life. Were the churches going to be centers of resistance or were they going to cooperate? Without embracing Marxist ideology, the "Three Self Movement" decided to support the new regime and join fellow Chinese in building a new society. Other Christians criticized the Three Self Movement believing that the ideology was manipulating it. Recently, the Chinese church created the Amity Foundation to promote health, education, and social welfare, and to symbolize cooperation with the state.

In Cuba, Christians disagreed over whether or not to participate in the local Committee to Defend the Revolu-

tion. Some Christians said, "We belong to another kingdom and will not participate in a sinful world." This meant
that these Christians were not in the voluntary brigade
which cleaned the streets, cut grain, or planted sugarcane.
They were criticized for benefiting from the environment
but not helping to improve it. Their lack of social involvement sometimes prevented them from getting good jobs or
places in the university. Other Christians cooperated. The
degree of cooperation affected what neighbors thought of
Christians. Christians in Cuba are struggling with how the
church is light, salt, and yeast to make society more
human.

In Nicaragua, evangelical pastors expressed their will-
ingness to cooperate with the government in programs that
benefit the people. They expressed this commitment with
the understanding that their participation was guided by
their loyalty to Christ.

The relationship of the church with the German Democratic Republic (East Germany) is instructive. Christians
here believe they can contribute to the construction of a socialist society through health, welfare, and peace concerns.
But the ideology is clearly in charge. It imposes limits upon
the church that affect its influence on society. The
churches are willing to support social change so long as
they are not asked to forgo criticism.

The churches in Eastern Europe do not agree on the
proper extent of cooperation. Some see the goals of social
change as similar to Christian ideals; some believe such
reconstruction is too political. Others have difficulty cooperating with a government that takes over church property
and teaches children that religion is superstition, a hin-
drance to progress in society.

In Taiwan some Christians support the government's policy of anticommunism and others oppose the government. There are blacks in South Africa who want to work within the system to bring reform and others who oppose any cooperation with the white regime.

Though critical participation may apply to many situations, its dangers are clearly seen in an ideology like apartheid. Christians must *oppose* an ideology that makes ethnicity and race the organizing principles in politics or that maintains power by dividing and ruling. The church must oppose an ideology that places limitations on freedom or denies blacks full participation. Christians must reject an ideology that allies nationalism with capitalism and that carefully distributes wealth, prestige, and power. The shape of that opposition is a continuing debate both within and outside the churches in South Africa.

Because of their stand on critical participation, Christians probably cannot avoid some disagreement. Churches hold different understandings of ideological conflicts. For example, some churches support illegal refugees that have been the victims of ideologies. Others do not. Given these different perspectives, we need to dialogue within churches and between churches and recognize the limits of cooperation. We affirm those values which come close to Christian values. Though we may share similar goals, we are not absorbed by the ideology. The church must be free for other important functions. One Chinese Christian said, "We may be committed to freedom and justice but our basic commitment is to God himself. He is the Lord of history."

The church must remember the "critical" aspect of critical participation. It dare not overlook the cautions and dangers. Some theologies have too quickly identified with an ideology, hastening to marry capitalism and Jesus or Marx and Jesus. The Lord will not allow himself to be absorbed by any ideological system. The gospel is easily distorted when brought under the control of a closed system. Christian symbols have been used as window dressing for ideologies. Christian faith dare never become a halo around unholy things. When faith is used for political ends, it becomes paralyzed.

Faith cannot be a power manipulated by an ideological system. Neither can it be made into an alternate ideology (e.g., Christian civilization). If we try to combine faith and ideology, we do violence to each, making them both heretical. Finally, faith sees ideologies from a different perspective than that from which the ideologies see themselves. Advocates of ideologies may not be happy with critical participation because it challenges their tendencies to absolute control and idolatry.

# CHAPTER 8

# *The Presence of the Local Church and Ideologies*

The presence of the church can be a powerful witness to specific ideologies. We see this clearly where ideologies have tried to limit or stamp out the church. Because the church points to a reality beyond the ideology, its presence threatens the ideology. But even if its presence provokes action, it needs to persist quietly.

*The Church as Alternate Community*

The church makes visible a new community, a different way of life. It demonstrates a community without class, race, or privilege, a sign of the new order in the midst of the old. This community of believers functions as a family, united through faith in Christ. By identifying with the people and their culture, it captures people's interest. For the church to have a critical encounter with the prevailing ideology, however, it must adapt itself creatively to each particular context.

Reflection and action in the local church clarify issues of

faith and ideology. Here fresh personal and corporate vision can create new forms of ministry. The church witnesses to another kingdom, God's rule, rather than developing a spirit of superiority or building its own empire. The church is a representative minority community through which God speaks to the world. As a community of hope, it provides a foretaste of the world to come. As a critical community, it reminds ideologies of their temporary character. Because the church is a subculture, it must guard against isolation, private piety, or a refugee mentality. Churches can easily turn inward in the midst of an ideology that is hostile to religion. Hostility can also tempt the church to disguise its identity, but authentic community must reject deception.

The local Christian community is receiving increased attention around the world. The Base Community movement in Latin America and elsewhere, for example, is growing in several ideological contexts. Churches in China have played key roles in the meeting of faith and ideology. In many places, the persecution of the institutional churches has revived the biblical pattern of the church meeting in the homes of believers.

## True Spiritual Communities

Christian communities are only authentic if members have experienced spiritual transformation. These communities must be rooted in Bible study, prayer, fasting, and renewal by the Holy Spirit. The Holy Spirit makes the necessary inner human changes that ideology aims at producing.

Renewed communities express a disciplined ethical life. The qualities of such a life include love, friendship, and hospitality both to those inside and those outside the church. These qualities also include honesty, integrity, openness, humility, dedication, compassion, peace, zeal, simplicity, sacrifice, and vulnerability. Justice, freedom, power, grace, sincerity, trust, patience, respect, acceptance, and fellowship are also important. Such Christian values are important to all ideological systems.

Reconciliation, forgiveness, and openness are important tests of spiritual transformation. The church as a sign of the reconciled community offers new ways of dealing with suspicion, alienation, injury, class struggle, hatred, and violence. People who experience oppression often turn against each other, as in South Africa. Michael Cassidy from South Africa, insists that the status quo is neither possible nor desirable. He noted that one cannot persuade advocates of apartheid to change their position. They need a Cornelius (someone who does good deeds). In the midst of the bad news of South Africa, he called upon the church to be good news—to be a community of hope, to build bridges, and then to cross them in reconciliation.

To be an example of renewal and reconciliation, the church must give up self-righteousness. Lifestyle is more important than institution. Involvement is more important than words. We are learning that consistent Christian behavior is more effective than confronting ideology. In China, one of the attractions of the church was the sense of mutual care, love, and compassion. Christians extended care even to those who had mistreated them and put them in prison. Christian love excelled the ideological slogan, "serve the people." The Chinese Revolution did more than isolate Christians; it brought them closer to their non-Christian neighbors.

## Communities of Transcendence

Human beings need transcendence (a relationship with that which is beyond). H. Richard Niebuhr wrote, "We are like migratory birds. We need to make periodic flights from the world that is seen to the world that is beyond our sight." The Christian religion provides more than escape, an opiate, or a sanctuary from earthly concerns. It reaches into spiritual realms beyond humanity and society.

Ideologies can't satisfy the human search for meaning in life nor answer questions about the end of life. Ideologies even create loneliness, alienation, disillusionment, or a spiritual vacuum. People hunger and thirst for meaning. They want to see beyond the ideology.

For example, we find a continuing interest in religion in Marxist socialist states. In the Soviet Union people want an alternative to atheism. Some Soviet writers decry the loss of spiritual values and morality. In the socialist countries of Eastern Europe, we find a renewal of religious life, despite Marxist orthodoxy. We see a revival of religion in China. Religion is not vanishing under socialism, even under systems that exert pressure. Rather, such pressure has caused the church to gain vitality and relevance, because Christian faith is by nature transcendent. State and party know nothing of—nor can they provide—the transcendent reality beyond freedom, justice, and materialism.

When an ideology is imposed on people, it can make them receptive to the gospel. It helps them evaluate the faith, reject distortions, and frees them to consider new options which fit their culture better. Atheism often ignites spiritual curiosity. Persons ask, "If there is no God, why is it necessary to speak against him so much?"

In Western secular societies, the religious quest is still

alive, even though secularism makes religion seem unnecessary. Secularism empties society of spiritual dimensions. Materialism does not satisfy. Now secularism is being
reevaluated. There are attempts to fill the emptiness with
religious belief and spiritual values. Religion has reap-
peared therefore—in either bizarre or authentic forms.

Ideologies are no substitute for religion. Wolfhart Pan-
nenberg said, "Religion will outlive every ideological
regime." The issue is not the death of religion, but the
renewal of Christian faith. There is a legitimate place for
religion. Religion can humanize life; it need not degrade or
cheapen it. One of the surprises is that young people are
searching for meaning in religion. No people can live
without the transcendent. Can the Christian community
attract the lonely and disillusioned who have lost meaning?

The worshiping community offers "something more,"
not only in the future, but a "something more" that affects
now. Worship testifies of a society within a society that ac-
knowledges no absolute truth but God. Prayer then becomes a form of witness. There is, however, a danger lurk-
ing there. Marxist governments often wish to confine the
church to the sanctuary and keep it from social action.
They would like to show that religion is merely a ritual—
that it is nothing more than a "fulfiller of needs."

The church must guard against this type of spiritual
isolation. While it is a sanctuary, it is also a sign. When
rightly understood, both sanctuary and sign threaten
ideologies.

## Organization, Leadership, and Nurture

In China the Cultural Revolution brought a harsh end to
the old forms of Christian institutions. They now have a

stripped-down form of the church in contrast to the elaborate church structures of the West. In Eastern Europe the church was forced to change its organization, self-understanding, and witness to society. Ideologies force us to be flexible, for putting our hope in institutions is a grave danger. We need to reexamine the nature of the gospel, the doctrine of the church, and the shape of church leadership. Local leadership development and self-reliance are essential in any given area.

When ideologies are hostile to Christian faith new sets of problems arise. For example, the government may take over church schools, hospitals, bookstores, and social institutions. Yet China has shown us that buildings and programs are not essential to church growth. The churches lost their buildings but grew through household cells. Christians may lose institutions, but they do not lose their knowledge of God and the Bible or the value of Christian fellowship.

Leadership training is important. Trained leaders can help the church to understand and deal more adequately with the issues that arise. Many churches are strong in experience but weak in teaching. Believers need to prepare themselves mentally and spiritually if they are to confront a new ideology creatively. Leaders need to prepare the church to counter the bombardment of propaganda and reeducation. Education of children, lay leadership (including youth and women), and discernment of spiritual gifts are crucial issues. These are especially important when leaders are being harassed or limited. They must be able to lead all age-groups to a deeper and broader understanding of the Bible and how it relates to all of life. We must avoid simple narrow piety that ignores the full gospel.

Patterns of ministry will vary when ideology is hostile toward the church. How does one make and nurture disciples in this kind of environment? Lifestyle evangelism may need to replace overt evangelism. No form of witness is itself a test of faithfulness. Quiet forms of witness by Christian presence often seem to be the most effective.

## Powerlessness and Suffering

The church does not seek power, but admits its weakness. This powerlessness is voluntary, not forced. Desmond Tutu of South Africa described the church there as a "failing community." Even faithfulness to the gospel does not guarantee success. Obedience may lead to rejection, suffering, or seeming failure. The Chinese church demonstrates what it means to live without power. As Simon Barrington Ward said, "If Christians in China today have any hope of offering another way to the many who are searching, it will be because they themselves have passed through an even deeper experience of death and coming to life again than has the nation."

Is the unparalleled openness to the gospel in China today related to the gospel's freedom from power? When the church is seemingly well-structured and self-sufficient, it may be least effective. When weak, vulnerable, and frail in the face of oppressive powers, it shows hidden resources of strength. One cannot separate faithfulness from the cross and suffering. The church frequently is tested and purged through criticism, misunderstanding, false accusation, discrimination, ridicule, persecution, and imprisonment.

Sometimes ideologies repress the church for religious reasons. At other times, harassment is for "alleged" political violations. Some criticism is justified and some of it is not. Where it is justified, the church must correct its mistakes. The church should not, however, seek suffering to test the limits of toleration or court martyrdom.

Repression and religious renewal are related. A Russian Christian proverb states, "If you pound a stake it may break. But if you pound it hard it may stick." Opposition can sometimes weaken the church. However, Uganda Bishop Festo Kivengere identified an important principle. He said, "Persecution never weakens the church; it is peace which weakens the church.... You have the strongest churches where you have the tightest pressure." A Yugoslav priest said, "When people stop dying for their faith, the faith starts dying."

Churches can claim no privileges, but they have obligations. If the cross symbolizes suffering, it also symbolizes hope. We must keep the cross and resurrection together. Death and resurrection are important themes in China. Grief can produce creativity. The church must give up the tendency to preserve itself. Self-denial and self-giving cannot be separated. This is how faith commends itself.

When suffering and oppression occur, the church should not rehearse the horrible past, but forgive and absorb the pain. The time of difficulties may only be a phase. Response to difficulty must take the long view to help shape the future. The task of the church is to celebrate hope. The church believes it will triumph. It is not, however, the victory of power but the triumph of weakness.

## *The Church: Ecumenical and International*

Ideologies may cause the church to be united or divided. Tensions can cause divisions within or between denominations. The church is not united in China, for there is the Three Self Church and others who prefer not to belong to it. In the Soviet Union there is a registered church and a nonregistered church.

Division among Christians occurs when some don't want to criticize the government and others feel compelled to do so. State pressure can cause distrust among believers. In repressive situations, Christians have sometimes betrayed other Christians for personal gain. Conflicts arise between Christians who accept state privileges and those who accept few such privileges. Sometimes ideologies seek to force unity upon the church in order to control it. Other times the ideology prefers disunity within the church because this promotes the ideology. For example, disunity in the South African churches can strengthen apartheid. The church can more easily be accused of being against the good of the people when divisions exist within it.

A divided church cannot effectively dialogue with ideology. Churches should discuss how ideology affects their expressions of faith. This dialogue should also take place among differing religious groups to work for greater unity. In China, a church has emerged without denominational tags. The China experience should challenge the church to move beyond such divisions. This could lead to a deeper unity and reconciliation among Christians despite the different ideologies with which they live.

Not only should Christians converse within an ideological system. Contact also needs to occur with the international church as well. Only then can we fully understand the global character of the kingdom of God. Some Christians defend capitalism; others defend socialism. Some Christians support a military dictatorship; others resist it. Some Christians think the church should not interfere in politics; others think noninvolvement is itself a political statement.

Diverse ideological commitments are not surprising. We should expect it in light of the church's engagement in a varied world. Our job is not to call each other names or hate one another. We need to exchange information, share our stories, expose ourselves to others, acknowledge our blindness, and correct our unfaithfulness.

When we agree to be tolerant, tension can lead to mutual enrichment. An example is Soviet Christians visiting North America, and North American Christians visiting the Soviet Union. My years of exposure to Africa help me to be more realistic about my ideological biases. Western Christians sometimes judge Chinese Christians more harshly for accommodating with their government than they judge their own accommodation with their governments. Bishop K. T. Ding says, "The goal of the Three Self Patriotic Movement is to make the church in China just as Chinese as the church in the United States is American."

Awareness of the international church helps us criticize the narrowness of our own ideology and prevents us from imposing it on others. While international contact is needed for fellowship and keeps the church from becoming ingrown, such contact dare not appear as foreign domination. Foreign ties can both threaten the self-reliance of the church and cause the ideology to suspect the church. Authoritarian governments fear manipulation by church agencies from countries whose ideology is hostile to their own. A common tactic of some governments is to sever all church ties with foreign lands.

Christians who live under a different ideology should

seek the counsel of local believers before acting or speaking for them. If they don't, they may create undue hardship for the people they are trying to help. The international church must show unity with and learn from believers who live in areas of ideological or political tension. The international church, however, should never act superior to nor threaten the local believers by its actions.

# CHAPTER 9

# *The Witness of the Church and Ideologies*

The church must do more than merely meet the needs of its members. It must witness and serve. The greatest is the one who serves, Jesus said. Ministry puts faith into action. Hungarian Protestants use the phrases *the servant church* and *theology of service*.

The church is a sanctuary but also a sign. Leaving its island of peace, it must move to the turbulent sea. Bearing the whole gospel, it must meet people where they are—physically, intellectually, culturally, politically, and spiritually.

It offers the message of salvation. It is a conscience for moral issues in the society. Leslie Newbigin insists that its style of living and speaking must regard all of life from the perspective of the cross.

The church does not call people out of the world nor seek to dominate the world by controlling its centers of power. It enables people to function in the world in ways which reflect the reality of Christ's presence.

## Witness of Social Action

The church believes in both personal and social ethics. It is not expert in social, economic, and political issues. It *is* competent in moral judgment. It clarifies social and political issues in light of the Christian ethic. As the church holds up a moral standard for the society at large, it serves as an effective vehicle for social change. While words are important, they are only understandable when supported by meaningful, symbolic action. Though faith is above ideology, it does not ignore visible social concern. This derives from a biblical vision rather than a specific program.

Social action is the counterpart to worship. The gospel we profess insists that the church must be salt and light. It must carry out social service programs whenever possible. Sometimes we focus so much on the church as opposed to the cultural values that we lose sight of the possibilities for social change. Han Wen Zao from China said the challenge facing the church today "is not atheism and materialism, but how to serve, to share, and to love."

Some ideologies do not welcome the church's involvement in social service programs. Capitalists and Marxists, for example, prefer that the church stay out of politics. Social activities are illegal in the Soviet Union and parts of Eastern Europe. (Eastern Germany is a major exception.) Marxists don't want Christians to have independent power to shape society since that threatens the working class and the party. Furthermore, if churches express social concern it contradicts what Marxists say about Christians being reactionary.

In fairness, we must state that the church was not socially active in the Soviet Union before the revolution.

Peter Dyck is a native of the Soviet Union and longtime employee of Mennonite Central Committee. He once asked someone in the council of religious affairs in the Soviet Union why the church is confined to religious activities. The reply was, "This had been the practice for 800 to 900 years."

The Soviet state has limited the church from doing social service and this has contributed to the heavy stress on piety and worship in the church. A Russian Christian said that some had learned the way of Mary, but had forgotten the way of Martha.

Can we add Martha's vision to that of Mary? For this, we need to give more attention to the social, economic, and political dimensions of the Bible. We should not address politics as though that were the whole gospel. On the other hand, to avoid politics is to neglect part of the whole gospel. Jesus' actions affected the Roman authorities.

The kingdom of God now and the kingdom of God to come enables present change and future hope. Our actions are signs of the kingdom. The kingdom vision strengthens our hope for social change. We dare not, however, become too optimistic about the political and social order. Christian action is different from political pressure. We do not coerce people. We plead and appeal. We do not try to create a new political order with God as leader.

Jesus did not create a perfect society and neither can we. We must be cautious about embracing causes, solutions, or utopian visions. We do what seems to be in line with God's will, but we are careful how we claim God's authority for our plans and programs. Leslie Newbigin points out the difference between commitment to a cause and commitment to a person. He says,

> When we separate the cause from the person, when we
> separate the kingdom from the king, we fall into ideology
> and we become victims of the law instead of bearers of the
> gospel. . . . The church is the sign of the kingdom only in-
> sofar as it points men and women to Jesus who is the one
> sign of the kingdom. (*Sign of the Kingdom*)

Concern for the present society does not cause us to lose
sight of eternal life. The vision for social justice points to a
final judgment against injustice. We see hope beyond the
ideological system. We are concerned for this world, not
*instead of* the next one, but *because* of it. Ideologies are
trying to make history turn out right. J. Howard Yoder says
Christians believe history will turn out right because Jesus
has come. We need not—indeed cannot—make history
turn out right.

We must hold social action in perspective with the
whole gospel. The oppressed will not be fully satisfied with
their eventual social or political liberation. Humans do not
live by bread alone. Bishop Ding of China has emphasized
that liberation is not the solution to the most important
questions, questions about the meaning of life, the meaning of humanness, and the end of life.

## Justice and Reconciliation

Concern for justice and human rights is not only to
preserve the church and its privileges. We are concerned
for religious liberties but also for civil liberties. Can Christians put others' rights ahead of their own? Can we become
an advocate for others?

The institutional church has usually sided with the
dominant class against the oppressed. The church has then

become an ideological tool for injustice. It is so easy to identify unknowingly with unjust systems. Can we demonstrate in practical life that belief in God does not cause us to be reactionary?

To ignore the demands of justice is to bring about injustice. We are so easily deceived by the belief that inaction is nonpolitical when, in fact, inaction supports the status quo. Neither apathy, despair, nor moral indignation is the right response to injustice. We must take sides in the struggle between life and death. Has not God taken sides?

A biblical perspective goes beyond ideological understandings of justice. Commitment to justice is essential, but our basic commitment is to God who loves the whole world.

*Love for All as the Motivating Factor*

Love keeps us from looking down on the disadvantaged. By our compassion for the oppressed and poor, we communicate our faith in a loving God who cares. We have a special concern for the less privileged but we do not limit our concern to them. We are concerned for all who are in God's image. We cannot therefore equate the kingdom of God with the coming of the poor to power.

The poor are not automatically righteous. Bishop Ding cautions us not to idealize the poor. The destructive Cultural Revolution in China grew out of the revolution of the idealized poor. Jesus loved the poor without hating the rich. God is concerned for the poor but it is important that both the poor and rich move toward Jesus. Christ did not give his life for just a few, select classes, but for all.

When love for all motivates us, we reject hatred of class enemies and violence, including violence caused by structures or revolutions. Revolution sometimes merely reverses the structures of idolatry. The oppressed then become the new oppressors. The revolutionary ideologies soon become the new regime. Revolution itself never removes the sources of alienation. Justice without conscience is dead and becomes demonic. Both alienation and liberation require reconciliation in its fullest dimensions—with God and with humans.

This is not "cheap reconciliation" which ignores the causes of conflict. We must be on the side of right. We must be for justice, peace, and reconciliation—in that order. There can be no enduring reconciliation without justice. Authentic reconciliation begins by taking a stand for righteousness, but such taking of sides in the name of Jesus refuses to hate the one who has done wrong. We must take some responsibility for the oppressor.

Class struggle regards the oppressor as a class enemy and nothing else. Christians believe the unique thing about the gospel is that Jesus Christ loves all persons equally. We cannot ignore, dismiss, or give up on anyone. The gospel regards people at a deeper level than ideologies. We do more than hate the oppressor and love the oppressed. We side with Christ against sin, whether in the oppressor or oppressed.

Is reconciliation not possible, then, until justice is fully done? What hope is there for whites and blacks in South Africa or for Jews and Palestinians? Are there any alternatives at all between hoping for liberation and resignation? Can there be any reconciliation at all on a smaller scale?

Does the church as the new community offer any hope? I believe it does. In the church we learn that repentance precedes reconciliation and that forgiveness is possible. In the church we can build fragile bonds of trust. The early Christian community included Barbarian and Scythian, slave and free, male and female, Jew and Gentile, even if these groups were not reconciled in the larger community.

I recently met an Arab Christian in Israel who was fellowshiping with Jewish believers in Jesus. When I acted surprised, he replied, "In Jesus, we are one." We should not despise authentic models of reconciliation on a small scale. They can help to point the way. But reconciliation within the Christian community should not keep us from ministries of justice and reconciliation in the larger society.

*Prophetic Witness*

The voice of the prophet must first focus inward. The church must admit its failures, some of which give rise to ideology. It must learn from past mistakes so as not to repeat them. The gospel must address the beliefs and actions of the church which have been too conditioned by ideology.

The gospel must also address ideologies to keep them honest and human. Since oppression thrives on lies, the church exposes injustice by declaring the truth. Churches often avoid such prophetic critique for two reasons. They may be too closely associated with the dominant ideology or they may be a minority seeking acceptance by the ideology. From its involvement in society the church is called to evaluate ideologies in light of the will of God. This requires sensitivity and courage.

Prophetic critique does not mean assuming a bitter or scathing attitude. We are passionate but loving. We confront, but work for a positive presentation of the gospel. As diplomatic prophets, we seek to build trust, not to embarrass. We choose carefully the particular areas we address rather than work on all fronts at once.

Our words may not be successful. They may, in fact, irritate the ideology without affecting policy. But the lone voice can keep the church from compromising and sometimes make an effective impact on the ideology. For example, the Christians had an impact on religious freedom in the Chinese constitution. Where public challenge to the government is illegal, consider Christian presence or actions that function as a sign. Mother Theresa is prophetic, more by example than by verbal criticism. She describes herself as "a little pencil in God's hands."

Sometimes, however, faithfulness will demand civil disobedience. There are times when we are called upon to act in obedience to God and not to human institutions.

The church must give attention to the way it communicates the prophetic word. It should not try to compete in the ideological field. It must respond to deep human anxieties and felt needs which only faith can satisfy. We must give our prophetic witness in such a way that people find it helpful in their lives. How people hear the gospel is important because of the alien character of some church doctrine. It is more important to find ways of telling the story in our context than to mouth slogans. Our communication will be shaped by cultures formed by ideologies.

We must adapt our expressions of faith to specific times and locations. The New Testament itself used contemporary language to express God's revelation. We need not avoid using ideological terms, such as *solidarity, justice, or freedom* if we modify the words or fill them with new meaning. We need to address issues that give rise to ideologies, to respond to questions ideologies ask.

The gospel has its own agenda. It asks questions. The gospel engages ideologies in respect to God, humans, evil, power, alienation, morality, justice, peace, human rights, community, freedom, liberation, reconciliation, meaning, death, hope, and transcendence. It is important to converse about these basic human aspirations.

Terms and strategies may overlap but meanings will differ and strategies will diverge. Although Christians address issues of concern to ideology, they do so from the perspective of Jesus Christ. We dare not allow ideologies to function as secular versions of salvation.

*People Politics*

Ans J. van der Bent in *Christians and Communists* suggests that we should apply "people politics" in the face of all ideologies. This stands in contrast to "power politics." According to Bent, people politics requires a "dove ethic" and "serpent politics." The latter requires discretion, prudence, and wisdom. But serpent politics without dove ethics is perverse and destructive. On the other hand, dove ethics without serpent politics is weak and foolish. We need to keep serpent and dove together. People politics requires faith, ingenuity, and endurance. We know how destructive power politics was in Hitler's Germany, in Pol Pot's Kampuchea, in Idi Amin's Uganda, in Afghanistan, and in Vietnam. Some ideologies emphasize people politics in names and slogans, but frequently play power politics.

People come before ideology, yet people happen to live within an ideological system. We must see people as people and not as capitalists, secularists, or communists. Not everyone in a Marxist society is Marxist as not everyone in a capitalist society is capitalist. Persons are more than a particular ideology, and we must meet them at the human level. An atheistic ideology does not create an atheistic society just as a Christianized ideology does not create a Christian society. We are people who think and act apart from impersonal systems.

To understand people, we must start with our common humanity. We must express our relationship with God in relationship with people. We invest in people rather than institutions. We are concerned for the whole person and help to prepare people for change. We empathize with people and their needs—sickness, pain, bereavement, death. We work for trust rather than fear, prejudice, or suspicion. To classify and stereotype people (e.g., as atheistic humanists) is not loving. Understandings of belief and unbelief should not separate us from our fellow citizens. It is better to talk together than to hate or even kill each other. Karl Barth reminds us that "the church stands for humans over against all systems and ideologies."

## Pilgrim Church

The church is on a pilgrimage. Its biblical examples include Abraham journeying from Ur, Israel escaping Egypt, the prophets turning from established Judaism, the disciples leaving their nets, and the apostles going from Jerusalem to Rome. Joseph Horomadka of Czechoslovakia called upon the church to become a "pilgrim church" representing Christ. It should give up political power and seek to minister in an unjust society.

Dietrich Bonhoeffer described the church as "without privileges." We need a realistic view of our social and historical situation. Can we concentrate on the opportunities we have rather than upon those that do not exist? Even when the church is "without privilege" it is not forsaken. Its very existence can be a witness. Loss of privilege does not bring an end to mission. Rather, it is an opportunity for renewal and for other forms of ministry.

Without privilege the church is on the margin. This should not, however, cause it to retreat to a ghetto of resignation or hopelessness. Even without status in society it has a message of life as it depends upon the gospel. The state can use power to propagate official ideology, but the powerlessness of the church can actually be an advantage. The gospel then appeals on the basis of a free offer, a free promise.

Under some ideological situations, the church is denied certain functions. It may lose its institutions, but it itself is not lost. The church as a body remains, both in its relationship with God and with each other. Being on the margin requires patience, yet the margin helps it to be a creative minority. It is like the ten righteous men of Abraham's day who had a good influence upon Sodom.

The church in pilgrimage takes the long view rather than the short one. In the face of frustration, it learns to be mobile and flexible. Like the Old Testament tabernacle it represents continuity and change. It is never uniform but varies with each new situation. In moments of crisis with ideology the church does not antagonize. When positive changes occur the church rejoices but does not gloat over its successes. As the church looks toward the future, it is drawn forward by hope.

# *Conclusion*

No part of the world is free from the power of ideologies. In every area the presence of ideology provides its own unique challenge to the church. In the first world, the church struggles with the loss of meaning because of prosperity and secular influences. In the second world, the church is concerned about the restriction and persecution of believers and for the limited role of the church in society. In the third world, the church agonizes over the meaning of justice amid poverty and oppression, caused largely by competing ideologies.

Mennonites seek to relate their theology to their encounter with ideology. We have a dissenting tradition. Anabaptists rejected Constantine's marriage of church and state, as did Marx and Engels later. As a free church, we distrust the power of institutions whether religious or ideological. We are not strangers to the prophetic role. Our concern for God's universal kingdom limits our loyalty to all human systems.

Mennonites accept the lordship of Christ, the authority of Scripture, voluntary discipleship, and separation from the world as the foundation for relating with society. The community of believers gives direction in a society shaped by ideology, avoiding the extremes of withdrawal or irresponsible action. Concerns for peace and reconciliation are particularly relevant in ideological conflicts. Anabaptists know that a suffering church can survive when it is free, flexible, and controlled by the Spirit.

Can we be faithful to our heritage? Or are we preoccupied with our identity—either struggling to be recognized, or not wanting to jeopardize a recently gained position of privilege?

We are called to a hope that is neither Christian triumphalism nor the naive optimism of ideologies. Our hope is in the kingdom of God—a kingdom that manifests signs of hope now and the promise of hope yet to come.

# Word List

**Allegiance**. The undivided loyalty supposedly owed by a citizen to his or her government or sovereign ruler

**Alienation** The separation of a person or one's affections from an object or position of former attachment, including self

**Apartheid**. A policy in South Africa that separates and controls groups of people with non-European background

**Authoritarianism**. The concentration of power in a leader or a few leaders who are not responsible to the people

**Bombardment**. The subjection of persons to constant and vigorous attack, either with words (propaganda) or moving objects, such as bullets

**Capitalism**. An economic system providing for private or corporate ownership of goods and services, with such investments determined by private decision rather than state control

**Collaboration**. The practice of assisting or cooperating with one's enemy, political or otherwise

**Concessions**. Favors granted by a government or other body in return for services given; points granted in an argument

**Consciousness**. The state of being aware of something within oneself or of being conscious of an external object, state, or fact

**Degenerating**. Sinking to a corrupt condition; moral decay

**Dehumanize**. To deprive of human qualities, personality, or spirit

**Discrimination**. The process of making a difference in treatment based on factors other than individual value or merit

**Elite**. A minority group that exercises power and maintains social superiority

**Ethnicity**. Affiliation or relationship to a group of people; ethnic quality

**Fanaticism**. Behavior marked by excessive enthusiasm and intense uncritical devotion

**Free Enterprise**. Freedom of private business to organize and operate for profit in a competitive system without government control beyond laws to protect the public interest; prices are controlled by supply and demand rather than government decree

**Ideology**. The collective guiding beliefs of a human group; a system of thought for structuring human society

**Imperialism**. The policy, practice, or intent of extending the power and rule of one nation over another, either by direct or indirect means

**Indigenous**. Originating in, growing, and living naturally in a particular region or environment

**Infallible**. Incapable of error

**Infiltrate**. To pass through or enter without notice for the purpose of overthrowing an established group or undermining a system of thought

**Intermingle**. To mix together

**Marxism**. The political, economic, and social principles and policies advocated by Karl Marx; includes the labor theory of value, the interacting forces of materialism, class struggle, and dictatorship of the middle class until the establishment of a classless society

**Modernization**. The act of making something modern

**Naive**. Marked by artless simplicity; lacking in judgment and worldly wisdom

**National Security states**. A system of government built on military power

**Nationalism**. Loyalty and devotion to a nation

**Orthodoxy**. Conforming to established doctrine, especially in religion

**Perpetuate**. To continue indefinitely

**Propaganda**. The spreading of ideas, information, or rumor to help or hinder an institution, a cause, or a person

**Propagation**. The spreading of something (as a belief) abroad or into new regions

**Rhetoric**. The art of speaking or writing effectively; flowery speech

**Secularization**. The process of changing a society from a religious foundation to a civil or secular one

**Socialism**. Any of various economic and political theories advocating collective or government ownership and administration of the means of production and distribution of goods; a system of society limiting private ownership

**Socialization**. The training of people for living with others by teaching them the values of society

**Sovereign**. One who exercises supreme authority within a limited area

**Sovereignty**. The freedom of individuals or institutions from external control

**Stereotyping**. Placing people in specific categories without evaluating their opinions, attitudes, or values; uncritical judgment

**Subversion.** The act of trying to overthrow or undermine a government or political system by persons working secretly within it

**Totalitarianism.** Centralized control by a few self-governing authorities; state-controlled rather than people-controlled government

**Transcendent.** Extending or lying beyond the limits of ordinary experience; being beyond human comprehension

**Transformation.** An act, process, or instance of change from one state of being into another; a complete change of attitude and action

**Triumphalism.** The belief that one religion or faith is superior to all others and that interreligious dialogue is unnecessary; religious imperialism

# For Further Reading and Study

Cox, Harvey, Ed. *The Church Amid Revolution.* New York, N.Y.: Association Press, 1967.

Eller, Vernard. *Christian Anarchy.* Grand Rapids, Mich.: Eerdmans, 1987.

Evans, Donald. *Communist Faith and Christian Faith.* Toronto, Ont.: Ryerson Press, 1964.

Leatt, James, Theo Kneifel, and Klaus Nurnburger, eds. *Contending Ideologies in South Africa.* Grand Rapids, Mich.: Eerdmans, 1986.

McGovern, Arthur F. *Marxism: An American Christian Perspective.* Maryknoll, N.Y.: Orbis Books, 1980.

Newbigin, Lesslie. *Sign of the Kingdom.* Grand Rapids, Mich.: Eerdmans, 1980.

Segundo, Juan Luis. *The Liberation of Theology.* Maryknoll, N.Y.: Orbis, 1976.

Van der Bent, Ans J. *Christians and Communists.* Geneva, Switzerland: World Council of Churches, 1980.

Verkuyl, J. *Contemporary Missiology.* Grand Rapids, Mich.: Eerdmans, 1978.

Yoder, John Howard. *The Politics of Jesus.* Grand Rapids, Mich.: Eerdmans, 1972.

# The Author

Calvin E. Shenk chairs Bible and Religion Department and professor of mission and world religions at Eastern Mennonite College.

He studied at Eastern Mennonite College (B.R.E.), Temple University (M.S. in Ed.) and New York University (Ph.D.). He has published articles in the areas of mission, church history, religion, ideology, and Christian presence. Among the committees on which he serves are: Overseas Committee of the Mennonite Board of Missions, Publication Board of the American Society of Missiology, and the Executive Committee of the International Association of Mission Studies.

He has pastored in Pennsylvania and served with the Eastern Mennonite Board of Missions in Ethiopia (1961-75). He has taught at Lancaster Mennonite High School, The Bible Academy (Ethiopia), Makane Yesus Seminary (Lutheran, Ethiopia), Haile Selassie I University (Ethiopia), Messiah College, Union Biblical Seminary (India), and Eastern Mennonite College and Seminary.

Calvin and his wife, Marie, are the parents of Douglas, Duane, and Donna. They live in Harrisonburg, Virginia, where they are active in the Park View Mennonite Church.

# PEACE AND JUSTICE SERIES

*Edited by Elizabeth Showalter and J. Allen Brubaker*

This series of books sets forth briefly and simply some important emphases of the Bible on war and peace and how to deal with conflict and injustice. The authors write from within the Anabaptist tradition. This includes viewing the Scriptures as a whole as the believing community discerns God's Word through the guidance of the Spirit.

Some of the titles reflect biblical, theological, or historical content. Other titles in the series show how these principles and insights are practical in daily life.

1. *The Way God Fights* by Lois Barrett
2. *How Christians Made Peace with War* by John Driver
3. *They Loved Their Enemies* by Marian Hostetler
4. *The Good News of Justice* by Hugo Zorrilla
5. *Freedom for the Captives* by José Gallardo
6. *When Kingdoms Clash* by Calvin E. Shenk
7. *Do Justice* by Lois Barrett

The books in this series are published in North America by:

Herald Press
616 Walnut Avenue
Scottdale, PA 15683
USA

Herald Press
117 King Street, West
Kitchener, ON N2G 4M5
CANADA

Overseas persons wanting copies for distribution or permission to translate may write to the Scottdale address listed above.